1

History of the Parish Church of the Holy Trinity St Andrews

History of the Parish Church of the Holy Trinity St Andrews

2012 Lulu Author Alexander Wynd All rights reserved

ISBN 978-0-9559789-1-3

Acknowledgements

Thanks are due to the following:

Fife Council St Andrews and Cupar libraries

University of St Andrews library Special Collections

Mrs. Vera Wynd for reading and comments

CONTENTS

Chapter 1

The Early Church

The history of the church in St Andrews is reputed to begin with St Regulus (St Rule) bringing the bones of St Andrew to a headland in Fife near the mouth of the River Eden. This is probably fictitious, as St Regulus was the Bishop of Senlis in France and it is unlikely that he came to St Andrews. Another bishop St Ringhail (a similar name to Regulus) came from Ireland and is not known to be associated with Scotland. However a monk form Iona, St Kenneth of Achadh-bo (517-600) came to St Andrews for a short period in about 570, but he left before 578. A church named Kilrymont was founded later. Kilrymont means the church on the King's Hill.

The bones of St Andrew (arm, kneecap, three fingers and a tooth) were transported from Hexham Abbey in the reign of King Angus (731-761) –did he steal them or did he buy them? A monastery was built on the site about 747 AD. It appears that the church rewrote history and invented the story of the bones of St Andrew to make up a fictitious connection with the apostles. One inhabitant of the monastery was King Constantine III, who abdicated after 43 years as king and joined the Culdee monastery as a monk in 843. The first church built was St Mary's on the rock, the foundations of this can still be seen today.

The first mention of Holy Trinity church in St Andrews was much later in about 1140 when the settlement became a burgh and the town needed a building for the spiritual welfare of the inhabitants. The site chosen was within the precinct of the East Gable of the cathedral and was served by a vicar, who was the deputy of the nominal rector. The church was endowed by Bishop Arnold (died 1162) and this was confirmed by Pope Alexander III in 1163. The church was inadequate and a petition was made to the pope to provide a second church in 1198. The church was consecrated in 1246.

At the same time the cathedral was started, the work commencing about 1160 and completed in 1318.

Sir William Lindsay of the Byres presented a site on 14 November 1410 in order to erect a new church in the centre of the burgh of St Andrews, which had greatly expanded. The site lay on the north side of Church Street and extended to the halfway line between Church Street and Market Street. The church was completed in 1412 and though greatly remodelled in subsequent alterations was substantially based on the same site. Bishop David de Bernham consecrated the new church in 1412, just as Pope Alexander XIII was granting the new university charter. The tower and west face of the church remains mainly as it was built.

There were altars. There was a donation by Mariota Burn of income from land in North Street to the altars of St Ninian and St Nicholas within the church.

The High Altar stood near the position of the present Communion table.

Choristers provided the music. In 1475 there were 30 priests of which 12 were choristers. The number was increased to 16 and in 1527 there were 10. There are still two choir stalls in the church with the arms of James IV and Gavin Dunbar (Archdeacon of St Andrews 1503-1518). Hymns were sung from fourteenth century and psalms were chanted in Latin. Originally the music was Plainsong (the Gregorian Chant) but there were improvements with a descant and from the fifteenth century polyphonic music.

Inside, the building would look as it does now except that it would be split halfway with a screen where the choir sat and the high altar stood below the great east window. There were a large number (at least thirty) of side altars. Daily services were held in the church. The Town Council in 1477 provided the money for an increase in worship on festival days.

The church had two bells, the great bell and the small bell. Bells were rung for the daily services at 5 am. In summer and 6 am in winter and also when the minister or reader was in the pulpit. Sir William Lindsay of the Byres, who was a great benefactor to the church, willed that bells be rung on the anniversary of his death in his memory. Bells were rung by a Sacrisan, who was paid twelve pence to ring the great bell. If he failed in his duty, he was to be put in the stocks. There

were also hand bells and the Bellman was paid three pence to ring the bell
through the town.

Chapter 2

Introduction

.With the establishment of the Kirk Sessions, starting in 1559, the basis of the organisation of the local church was established. Images had been demolished and the main part of local church worship was the sermon. The Bible was available in English, not Latin, but few could read. Hence, the Reformers were keen to have schools, where the people could read the Bible in their own language. The provision of the clergy was a problem as many of the former Roman Catholic priests were uneducated and it took time for a proper ministry to be established. The provision for the poor was another problem, as the nobles had stolen most of the old church endowments. The government of the church was also a problem, as King James VI did not wish to have a General Assembly of ministers (elders came later) but preferred to have bishops which he could control. The ministers led by Andrew Melville had an ongoing dispute with James VI about the control of the church and the organisation of the local church had not been resolved when James succeeded to the throne of England and Wales in 1603.

The Church in 1559

By the mid sixteenth century, the church was in a sorry state. The cathedral was dilapidated; the leadership of Archbishops, Bishops and monks were greedy and corrupt. The nobles had stolen all the money, which should have been paid to the parish clergy. The parish clergy were poor, and they also were uneducated. The burghs had their own churches and ministers, like Holy Trinity, so an alternative church was already present. The church was Roman Catholic until 10 June 1559, when John Knox preached in Holy Trinity. The subject of his sermon was "Christ cleansing the temple" and this stirred up the audience. The pulpit on which he preached is in the University, having been sold when the church was refurbished in 1800. The effect of the sermon was that the congregation decided to remove the altars and these were stripped by the population on 14 June 1559. John Knox made sure that the mob only removed treasures and relics and left the cathedral alone. The cathedral fell into decay and neglect and this dereliction was not due to the populace vandalising it, but to sheer neglect. Knox did his utmost to protect the priests. Archbishop Hamilton left St Andrews. All the altars used for prayers for the dead were thrown down. The only remains of the catholic regime was a mutilated Madonna.

The Reformed Church

Two of the three bishops of the old Church of Scotland joined the new reformed church. The laity were in control. Congregations had the power of electing elders and deacons to form a Kirk Session along with the minister. The Kirk Session minutes begin in July 1559. The minister was to be chosen by the congregation, but subject to the Kirk Session.

Superintendents were appointed to make up for the shortage of ministers. The old bishops were allowed to retain their bishoprics and most of the revenues but they did not perform the functions that the bishops performed before the Reformation. In 1571 a number of the former bishops had died. The church wanted their positions abolished and the revenues appointed for the support of ministers. The nobles did not like this, so the nobles took on the bishoprics themselves so that they could steal a portion of the revenues. After some negotiation and intimidation, a joint solution was found that the bishops should remain until the King achieved his majority. The bishops should only be chosen from proper ministers and they should have no greater power than superintendents and should be subject to the General Assembly.

Wynram

A man called Wynram was elected Superintendent of Fife, Forfar and Strathearn on 13 April 1561. The aim of this appointment was not to replace the old Bishops and Archbishops, but to make sure that the church was functioning, as the clergy coming from the old Roman Catholic church were uneducated and ill equipped to be parish ministers. Wynram resigned on 6 March 1571, but his resignation was not accepted. He died and was buried in St Leonard's chapel.

John Douglas

In 1572 John Douglas was appointed as the first post-Reformation Archbishop of St Andrews. The appointment was irregular. John Douglas eventually became too old and ill to continue as bishop. He was taunted as "a minister who could not preach." Eventually, he made a last effort and died in the pulpit in 1574. He was buried in the public cemetery without a memorial stone.

The first General Assembly of the Church of Scotland met in December 1560. It was comprised of ministers and 40 were present.

John Knox along with five collaborators drafted the Scots Confession, which was replaced by the Westminster confession of 1644. They also compiled the book of Common Order 1562, which was eventually replaced by the Westminster directory of 1643. The book of Common Order was a book containing details of the organisation of the church, including the Sacraments, marriage, and funerals, visitation of the sick, excommunication, public repentance, absolution, and a General Fast. The order of the Sacrament of Holy Communion was to follow the pattern laid out in 1 Corinthians 11. Baptism was to be administered after the sermon in the face of the congregation. The election of elders and deacons was to take place annually (this was copied from the Kirk Session records of St Andrews). The Kirk Session was empowered to watch over members including the minister. The Book also said that the Lords prayer, the Apostles Creed and the Ten Commandments should be repeated at every service. The congregation was allowed to share in the worship by singing Psalms. The Lord's Supper should be celebrated as often as the congregation should think it expedient.

A national Parliament met on 17 August 1559 and the Scots Confession received parliamentary sanction. The authority of the Pope was abolished. The rights of the Catholic Church were annulled and the saying of mass was made a criminal offence. Queen Mary was an absentee in France at this time.

Episcopacy and the king

Archbishop Hamilton was hanged for treason in 1571 and John Douglas was appointed in his place. Bishops came into being in 1572, by the Crown nominating the candidates. Regent Morton appointed more bishops between 1572 and 1576. These bishops were called "tulchan" Bishops, after the word for a calf stuffed with straw to make the cow give up her milk. The meaning was that the bishops were "empty vessels" and were without any power. The General Assembly held them under its discipline. The General Assembly of 1572 criticised the appointment of bishops.

Andrew Melville

After the death of John Knox in 1573, Andrew Melville became one of the leaders of the Church of Scotland. He was born at Baldovy near Montrose in 1545. His father was killed at the Battle of Pinkie. He was educated at St Andrews University, studying at St Mary's College in 1559, in 1564 at Paris and in 1566 at Poitiers. He became minister in Geneva at a time when there were great reformers there, Beza and Calvin. He was asked to go back to Scotland by the Regent and he became Principal of the University of Glasgow in 1575 and became Principal of St Mary's College in St Andrews in December 1580, due to the direct intervention of James VI. He was five times Moderator of the General Assembly of the Church of Scotland, April 1578, April and June 1582, June 1587 and May 1594. As well as taking a prominent part in the affairs of the Church of Scotland and being the architect of the organisation in the early years, he was frequently a preacher and also was an elder of Holy Trinity Church. He fell foul of King James VI, had to flee to England 1584-1586. He came back to St. Andrews. He led a deputation to King James VI in 1596. After leading a deputation to King James VI in London, he was put in the tower of London 1606-1611, although he had committed no offence. He was released and spent the latter days of his life on the continent at the University of Sedan. He died in 1622.

Andrew Melville in 1574 wanted rid of the Bishops. He proposed a system of church courts with ministers and elders to form a Kirk Session and above them Presbytery, Synod and General Assembly. This system was adopted in 1575. In the same year the General Assembly stated that bishops were to be pastors of a single congregation although they had oversight of a number of congregations.

Problems arose between the Church and the King when King James started to rule on his own accord in 1583. These problems were at the national level as the king wished to control the church and he saw the Episcopalian system with Archbishops and Bishops directly under himself controlling every aspect of church life. However during his reign, James was not interested interfering with the actual church services, but only with ecclesiastic politics. This did affect the church of the Holy Trinity as there was now no cathedral and the bishops used the church as their cathedral.

There was a Second book of Discipline in 1578. It claimed that there was a distinction between civil and ecclesiastic government. It was really a declaration of the independence of the church. The General Assembly claimed the right to examine **Patrick Adamson** (1537-1592), who was nominated Archbishop of St Andrews.

Patrick Adamson was a gifted man but he was not sufficiently balanced in his judgement and probably it was impossible to please both the King and the General Assembly. He was a Royalist and at an early stage his commentary on Timothy was suppressed (by the Act of Parliament of 1563). He wrote a catechism in Latin in four volumes. He also wrote sacred poems, which were edited after his death. Adamson agreed to obey the General Assembly. Regent Morton was furious and vowed to hang a dozen ministers. The bishops had to submit to the General Assembly and in July 1580 the office of bishop was deemed unlawful. However Parliament passed the "black acts" where the king's superiority was assented and bishops were given power again. In 1585, Archbishop Adamson was excommunicated, but in 1586, the excommunication was annulled by the General Assembly. Bishops were to be the moderators of

Presbyteries. In 1587, Parliament passed an act of the annexation of the revenues of bishoprics and abbeys.

Kirk Sessions

The first Kirk Session register started on 27 October 1559. The Kirk Session consisted of twelve elders and seven deacons. The deacons were elected yearly. The first election was held on 1 October 1561. The office bearers met weekly until 1568, usually on a Thursday at 2 p.m. The meetings were of both elders and deacons. The deacons were not members of the Session, but were present to supervise financial arrangements. However in practice they attended Session meetings and took part in discussions even on non-financial matters. The task of the elders was to report on the state of morals and the necessities of the poor.

The meetings were called ministry at first and then the Session. There were yearly elections until 1600. Often the magistrates were elders. Some of the university lecturers were also elders to set an example. Church law decreed that elders and deacons should be chosen by the voice of the congregation. Where the elders were chosen by the Kirk Session, the people retained a right to veto the appointments. The people also retained a right to add to the list of nominees. This right was exercised upon the serving of the edict.

The Kirk Session examined ministers, elders and deacons, by the device of removing them from the meeting one by one, where the others would conduct a trial of judgement upon them by remainder. The members could be commended, admonished or rebuked.

In 1571 the elders included John Douglas as rector, nine other elders and eight deacons. In 1572 the Kirk Session included John Rutherford (Provost of St Salvators), John Wilkie (Principal of St Leonards) Archibald Hamilton (New College), twelve elders and eleven deacons.

In 1590, Archbishop Adamson wrote an appeal to the King in a Latin translation of the books of Jeremiah and Lamentations but the ungrateful King ignored the appeal. Archbishop Adamson was very poor and needy and was only rescued by the Melvilles, his opponents.

Parliament.

During 1584, Parliament declared James VI as Head of the Church of Scotland. It gave the king jurisdiction over excluded cases. The courts and assemblies of the church were dissolved and bishops were to be appointed.

In 1589 there was another U-turn and the king agreed to make provision for the church. In 1592, the King made a sudden change of direction and Parliament recognised Presbyteries and suspended the bishops. The General Assembly was given the right to meet. During this time the Kirk Session nominated members as elders to the Presbytery and this was against Church Law according to the Acts of the General Assembly.

Melville and the King met in 1596 to reconcile their differences.

Ministers
Adam Heriot

The first minister was Adam Heriot (an Augustinian canon), who was inducted in 1559. He went to Aberdeen sometime before July 1560. He died in 1574.

John Knox

The second quoted minister was John Knox in 1559-1560. John Knox was a student at St Andrews University. He was ordained in 1536. He was sword bearer to George Wishart and was a slave in the French galleys. He was rescued by the Earl of Somerset and served as a chaplain in Berwick. He was one of the authors of the black Rubric, which stated that members should not kneel when receiving communion. He arrived in St Andrews in November 1559 and left in April 1560 and he acted as Minister at least some of that time. He was inducted into St Giles on 7 July 1560. John Knox also preached in Holy Trinity on his retiral between 1571 and August 1572 on some Sundays. Andrew Melville heard him preaching in St Andrews on the prophecy of Daniel and said he took notes for ½ hour and then just listened to the sermon, as Knox was so powerful a preacher. Melville said that Knox was like to ding the pulpit in blads and come down amongst the people. On the last Sunday when he visited St Andrews, he preached in Holy Trinity but was so weak that he had to be carried up to the pulpit by his servant, Richard Ballanden along with another servant. John Knox died in Edinburgh in November 1573.

Christopher Goodman

Christopher Goodman BA MA BD was the third minister. He was born in 1519 and studied at Oxford and was at Strasbourg, Frankfurt, and Geneva. On the encouragement of John Knox, he became minister of Ayr in November 1559. He was inducted to St Andrews in 1560. He was a member of the first General Assembly and also the General Assemblies in 1562, 1563, 1564 and 1565. He went to England in 1565 and died in 1603. He wrote a Commentary on Amos, and helped in the translation of the Coverdale Bible. He also wrote, "How supreme Powers ought to be obeyed by their subjects and whenever they may be lawfully by God's Word be disobeyed and resisted."

Robert Hamilton

Robert Hamilton became the fourth minister in 1566. He was Moderator of the General Assembly in 1571 and 1579. Hamilton, at the end of his ministry had allowed his pastoral duties to slip and in particular did not "give reproofs" to the inhabitants of St Andrews. He was assisted in his preaching by Archbishop Adamson, who was often absent and so Andrew Melville, who was the Principal of St Mary's College, was obliged to preach in his place. Robert Hamilton was deprived of his provostry in 1579, but it is not clear why this happened, but it may have had something to do with his health. He died in 1581. He also had the services of a reader George Black in 1579.

As an example of the Kirk Session 's work at this time, Adam Masterton quarrelled with Agnes Boyd, his wife. The matter was referred to the Kirk Session. The pair was reconciled. The man accepted her as his lawful wife.

Adam, at the desire of John Douglas (Bishop 1573-1574) kissed and embraced Agnes and clove to her.

When Robert Hamilton died in April 1581, Principal Andrew Melville of St Mary's College and James Melville, who was Professor of Oriental Languages, conducted the services. But Andrew Melville was anxious that the congregation obtained the services of a competent minister to conduct services and carry out pastoral duties. With a request from the Kirk Session of St Andrews and the consent of the General Assembly, they procured the services of a well-known minister, Robert Pont.

Robert Pont

Robert Pont (1524-1606) was a native of Culross. He may have been minister between 1581-1583. He was minister of St Cuthbert's in Edinburgh, but he was willing to come to St Andrews. He could not secure a stipend as the Earl of March, the former prior and pensioners of the Abbey with the connivance of the Town Council confiscated the money. The Earl of March was charged with colluding with the Town Council and spending the stipend money on golf, archery and "good cheer." Robert Pont became Moderator of the General Assembly. He left with the approval of the General Assembly. It is not clear whether Robert Pont was ever in St Andrews, although nominally he was the minister there. It was proposed that either the Principal of Glasgow University or the Principal of Aberdeen University would become the new minister, but King James vetoed this.

Church Vacancy

During this period between the death of Robert Hamilton in April 1581 and the installation of John Rutherford in July 1584, Patrick Adamson (the Bishop) and George Black and Thomas Wood (readers) conducted the services together with Andrew and James Melville of the University of St Andrews.

When the Presbytery of St Andrews released James and Andrew Melville from their duties at Holy Trinity, two of the town bailies wrote a disgruntled paper making disrespectful assertions on the Presbytery, which was read in the church by the precentor. (He probably had little option). Unfortunately the precentor was in poor health afterwards. The two bailies were summoned before the General Assembly and were ordered to do public penance before Andrew Melville in the church, possibly having to sit on the penitents stool for several Sundays- imagine the glee of the populace seeing their town councillors humiliated! However the councillors did their penance and became "better conditioned thereafter."

What were the problems between the church and the town council? It was all a matter of money; precisely who obtained the revenues from the old church lands and the savings to the Town Council if they did not have to pay for a minister.

One Sunday during the vacancy, Melville preached and "gave reproofs" to the congregation. Melville was really disgusted at the behaviour of the inhabitants of St Andrews and really gave his reproof for their conduct in very plain terms. Melville also attacked those who obstructed the settlement of the next minister (for financial reasons). Most of the people were happy with Melville, but a few people were not pleased with what he said. These included the Provost and the bailies. The Provost of St Andrews in particular did not like the sermon and rose in the middle and walked out muttering imprecations against Melville. He threatened to set fire to Melville's house and chase him out of town. The bailies put placards at the gate of the College. The Provost was summoned before the Presbytery of St Andrews to account for his behaviour.

On 15 February1584, Andrew Melville had a summons to appear before the Privy Council on account of a sermon preached in Holy Trinity in January 1584. The sermon was based on the text with which Daniel reminded Belshazzar of the history of his father, Nebuchadnezzar. He deduced from the text the divine mercy and judgement to all ages, Kings, princes and people. Melville denied that he said that the king was unlawfully promoted to the crown or that he made references to the king's mother (Mary Queen of Scots). However he did say that Kings owe their exaltation to God and due to the infirmities of human nature, they are extremely apt to forget this truth. It is not surprising that the King was not happy with what Melville did say, as he was an absolute monarch. Melville received attestations of his good behaviour from the University, the Presbytery and even the Town Council to no avail. King James and the Earl of Arran were angry with him and were out for revenge, no matter what defence he made. The Privy Council sentenced him to be jailed. Melville fled to England and was there between 1584 and 1586,

John Rutherford

John Rutherford was Robert Pont's successor between July 1584 and October1585. When he was minister of Kemback, the king asked him "Wouldst thou be minister of St Andrews." Rutherford replied "Yes sir, but shame for me if I do not do my duties." The King said, "Shame for thee and the devil receive thee too if thee do not. Go thy way." Rutherford died of the plague in October 1585.

Patrick Adamson

While Rutherford was minister, **Patrick Adamson**, was Bishop. He had been appointed Archbishop in 1575. In 1586, Adamson had been excommunicated by the Synod of Fife for heresy. The General Assembly remitted the sentence as illegal. However he was excommunicated again in 1588, but the sentence was again remitted. Despite his excommunication, he was intending to preach at the service in Holy Trinity on the Sunday. A large number of people, who usually went to worship at Holy Trinity, went to the St Mary's chapel to worship, as they did not wish to listen to a sermon by an excommunicated minister. One individual who saw the crowd going to the university chapel, told Patrick Adamson that a number of gentlemen, who were dissatisfied with him, were going to the church to take him out of the pulpit and hang him. The bishop was afraid and took refuge in the belfry. He refused to come down and the Magistrates had great difficulty in persuading him to come down. Eventually they did persuade him by promising to escort him home safely. The General Assembly reinstated Patrick Adamson as Bishop on 10 May.

Later, when Adamson preached, a large number of people went to the theological college to worship instead of listening to him. Adamson was so annoyed that he managed to obtain an order from Parliament that the worship in the university chapel should be in Latin in order to prevent the mass of the people from going there to worship.

Robert Wilkie

Robert Wilkie was minister from June 1586 until September 1590 when he became Principal of St Leonard's College. After becoming Principal, he was elected as an elder of Holy Trinity in January 1590 until January 1591 and in 1593 and 1594.

During his ministry in 1587, the ministers were asked to pray for the life of Mary Queen of Scots. The ministers were glad to do this as they did not wish to see her executed, but it was all in vain.

There was a vacancy in 1590 and the Presbytery ordered that the vacancy be filled speedily. This caused great offence to some of the population (the Town Council).

Eventually Melville managed to have two faithful and industrious ministers appointed.

David Black

David Black (1590-1597) was the first of the two ministers. Black had zeal and energy but got no help and was appointed as minister of Auchinleck. In April 1593, the General Assembly said that he should discharge his duties of an ordinary pastor and nominated Robert Wallace as colleague. On 15 September 1593, they finally accepted the ministry and the town was divided into two parts and subdivided into seven districts. Black gave conditions to his ministry on 12 December 1593. The conditions were as follows: The Black and Wallace ministry should be established and the magistrates should with faithful diligence obtain obedience to the word. During the years of their ministry there was a more searching and thorough reformation than ever before.

The main sin was fornication. The practice was that fornicators would be fined 40 shillings. But the new reformation was that the penalty for the sin would be 40 pounds, which would be donated to the church's fund for the poor. The alternative punishment was imprisonment for eight days with the food bread and small drink, thereafter to be presented to the market cross bare headed and stand for two hours. On the second offence, the fine would be doubled or a double imprisonment with bread and water only. And the head would be shaved before standing at the market cross. On the third time, the fine would be one hundred pounds, imprisonment with bread and water, ducked (into the sea) and banished from the town. The full penalty was not always applied.

Adulterers were put into the jougs and rotten eggs were thrown at them. An adulterer was then ducked and banished and also had to face an ecclesiastic punishment on the penitential stool.

The results were that in the five years of Black's ministry, only five cases of adultery were found (not all relevant to these years) and in the last year of his ministry there were no cases at all.

As well as sexual offences there were cases of Sabbath breaking and penalties for these. The worst Sabbath breakers were those who were absent from public worship. He also condemned those who went to Leuchars for a drink on the Sunday. The attendance at worship increased. On one Sunday there was no preaching at St Leonards and the crowd was so great that part of the intending worshippers had to be sent to the University chapel for worship.

Black was insistent that proper provision be made for the poor. He also insisted that the elders attend to the manners of the people.

The Kirk Session forbade the members to bring guns or swords to the meetings of the Session and not to carry them to the stool of repentance.

The Kirk Session said that members must repeat the Lord's prayer, the Creed and Commandments or be fined 40 shillings. Marriages could only be celebrated on Fridays, Sundays and Wednesdays. The poor were to be funded by the payments from transgressors, alms, compulsory contributions, wills, altarages (i.e. church collections) and vow-silver (i.e. promises of money to be donated to the church). A hospital was also provided. The members of the parish, who were sick, were noted by the elders, who were diligent in visiting them and the elders had to tell the ministers who visited and comforted them. (May 1596) Burials were not to be held at the time of the sermon.

Communion procedure.

Tokens or tickets were given out. There was also to be an examination before the yearly communion. The town communion was held between July 1584 and July 1589 at yearly intervals. Thereafter it was held on 23 March 1593, 1594, May 1595, April 1596, October and December 1597 and July 1598. The country communion was held on August 1583, August 1586, August 1588, June/July 1589, July 1590, August 1598, 1599, February 1600 and August 1600.

The office bearers could be disciplined as well. A deacon was stuck off the office bearer's list for being an evil payer of debts, an aged elder for adultery and a deacon for speaking against the magistrates. In 1599 some of the office bearers missed the Session meeting because they were playing golf. The Session was not against golf, but only against Sabbath playing and office bearers missing Session meetings because of it.

Black is worthy of being remembered as one of the best ministers that St Andrews have had in their history. He had no easy task with 3000 regular communicants. At the end of his ministry there were no beggars in the town, the place was quiet on a Sunday and there was a hospital for the sick.

In 1595, Black had a problem with William Balfour of Burley, who had possession of the manse assigned to the minister and refused to give it up at the minister's bidding. Burleigh went to the court accusing the minister of reviling the late Queen in his sermons. David Black and Andrew Melville were summoned to a meeting in Falkland Palace called by King James. The meeting was irregular consisting of members of the Privy Council and some ministers and matters became heated. James Melville acquainted the Earl of Mar with the real circumstances of the case and persuaded him to mollify the king. David Black satisfied the king that these allegations were false and the case was dismissed after Balfour sank on his knees as a suppliant for mercy.

David Black again was in trouble. He was accused, apparently at the instigation of the English ambassador of having preached that all kings were children of the devil, Queen Elizabeth was an atheist and the nobles were godless enemies of the church and the Privy Council were buffoons and cormorants of no religion (Cormorants were greedy birds, a very apt description of the Privy Council). The Privy Council proceeded against David Black, making allegations about these comments. Black appeared before the Council on 18 November 1596 and declined the jurisdiction of any civil court, if his offence was deemed ecclesiastical. In his defence the city of Edinburgh pastors, Pont and Bruce and the church assisted him. The Committee accepted Black's statement as a statement for the whole church. 300 ministers signed a declaration that the rights of the church were compromised by this case. Black was being made a scapegoat because of problems with certain lords especially the Earl of Huntly (a prominent Catholic Lord, who wished to restore the Papacy).

Despite this, the King and the Privy Council proceeded against Black and found him guilty, despite a recommendation of his character made by the Provost and citizens of St Andrews. Eventually David Black was removed from the church of St Andrews in October 1596 "without any form or process" and banished beyond the Tay water. On being reconciled with the king, he became minister of Arbirlot in 1602 and was there for six years.

King James visited St Andrews and attended Holy Trinity Church. He interrupted the minister, Robert Wallace and told him to stop his sermon. Andrew Melville, who was present, rebuked the King and threatened him with the Judgement of God if he did not repent of his actions.

There were a number of ministers of the second charge after 1588.

John Auchinleck

John Auchinleck MA was elected by the members of his parish to be minister on 15 December 1589 and he was translated to Largo in 1593.

Robert Wallace

Robert Wallace 1593-1598 was the other faithful minister. He was minister of Leuchars and was admitted to Holy Trinity on 27 May 1593. He accused the Secretary of State (John Lindsay) of bribery, partiality and injustice in the excommunication of witnesses in Black's process. The Secretary of State was willing to pass over the offence, but he was instigated to prosecute. Wallace declined the judgement of the commissioners and was removed from St Andrews and was also suspended on 11 July 1596. He was minister at Glenluce in 1599. He became minister of Tranent on 10 December 1602.

David Lindsay

David Lindsay (1597-1606) followed him. He was inducted on 17 August 1597 and was translated to Forgan in 1606.

Robert Yuill

There was a third charge between 1593 and 1620. The only minister listed was **Robert Yuill** in 1593-1603. He was appointed Moderator of the presbytery but this did not take off.

Witchcraft.

One of the problems of the church between 1560 and 1667 was the supposed cases of witchcraft.

The role of the Kirk Session was a preliminary one in cases of witchcraft or even charming. These cases were dealt with in the same way as other cases of ungodly behaviour such as Sabbath breaking or having illicit sex. The minor cases dealt with included cursing or charming or consulting a known witch. The Kirk Session reproved these people by making them attend the church and giving them a good telling off during the service in front of the congregation. The accused said sorry and they would not do it again. However serious cases of witchcraft were dealt with by the magistrates or the Privy Council (e.g. the cases of 1569) or the Regent (1569) or even by the King (King James VI was too keen to expose witches).

Sometimes persons would approach the Kirk Session to have their names cleared of accusations of witchcraft.

A complete list of known cases of witchcraft is in the appendix.

Two cases of people who tried to help accused persons stand out. When Margaret Smith was accused of witchcraft, her husband was not involved. Nevertheless, he was afraid for his wife's safety and the couple fled from St Andrews for her safety. Margaret Balfour's husband rode a horse on a Sunday to see Lord Burley to plead for the safety of Margaret Balfour, who was accused of witchcraft. The outcome is not known but the young man was reproved by the Kirk Session for breaking the Sabbath.

Sometimes an accused witch's trial was not proceeded with as in the case of Agnes Melville in 1588 and sometimes a warning by the Session was sufficient e.g. Bessie Robertson (1585).

In a civil trial if a witch was found guilty he or she would be hanged e.g. William Stewart (Lord Lyon King of Arms) in 1569, or strangled and then the corpse was burnt as in the cases of Nic Melville (Nick Niven) 1569, Richard Bannantyne 1575, Elspot Gilchrist 1595, Janet Lochequair 1593, Agnes Melville 1595 and Bessie Mason 1644. Sometimes we only know that a person was accused of witchcraft, but we do not know the outcome of the case. It is interesting the best defence was a jury packed with relatives. In only eight cases out of twenty-seven named persons do we know that the person was executed, but there would likely have been more people condemned of whom we know nothing?

Church buildings in the early seventeenth century

Some changes had to be made to the church to accommodate the changed beliefs and this was done. A new pulpit was made and this is now in the University. Upstairs there were galleries to accommodate such people as the Town Council and the heritors and there would have been benches for the majority of the congregation. There was a gallery dated 1580 called the sailors loft. (It was sold to the burgher church in 1798). Some of the ordinary people sat on stools (e.g. in St Giles Jenny Geddes threw her stool at the preacher). There was also a Communion aisle where the congregation sat when partaking of Communion (on the site of the present Sharp Aisle). There was an entrance porch and a small vestry on part of the site of the present Playfair aisle.

Office bearers duties at about 1600

The new elders had to attend to the church matters and were fined for non-attendance at the weekly Kirk Session meetings and also fined if they were late or left the meeting early. The elders were elected for one year only. The congregation had the right to veto the nominations by the Kirk Session and to propose additional elders. There was a variety of business, but the Kirk Session only had powers to give a telling off in front of the congregation. There does not seem to be a clear line between the power of the Kirk Session and the power of the magistrates, who alone could imprison people. However there were always at least three Baillies on the Kirk Session so they had a lot of civil power.

One of the duties of the Session was to adjudicate in divorce cases.

Often a deserted husband would sue for divorce on the grounds that his wife had deserted him. In one case the wife had disappeared to Denmark and married another person. In these cases, the divorce was granted. In other cases there was the problem of the unmarried mother who had a baby. The accused man would say that it wasn't his and witnesses were called. The main purpose was a humanitarian one, to find support for the woman and baby. Adulterers were often ordered to go before the congregation on a repentance stool.

Another case was dealing with a petition from a jilted bride and the Kirk Session was asked to make the offending man marry her.

Other instances before the Session involved Sabbath breaking. Sometimes a fine was imposed, which went to help the poor of the congregation.

Other cases involved drunkards, who had to sit on the repentance stool for a number of Sundays.

There was also the case of the husband, who injured his wife.

In some cases the offender was placed in the jougs at the market cross.

In serious cases the magistrates could order banishment from St Andrews.

Weddings were usually held on Sunday before the congregation. There was an appeal before the Kirk Session to allow a wedding to be held on a Wednesday for special reasons and this was allowed. The General Assembly made a decree in 1579 allowing marriages on any day of the week.

The tower at the West Side of the church was used as a prison. The Kirk Session record stated "that the tower was the chosen prison house of the wicked. Nor could one hope to get free until the beadle, worthy man had his two shillings. Many a woman climbed the steep stair to the dreary prison in the steeple so remote and solitary and one poor soul terrified by a storm of thunder perchance had to be released on bail."

From 1560 until 1589 there was a single minister assisted by a reader for the whole parish including a huge landward area, but in 1589 a second charge was made. The minister's stipend was a problem although some of the vicarage teinds were given to assist the payments.

Chapter 3
Seventeenth century
Introduction

During the seventeenth century, with accession of James VI to the English throne in 1603, the Government policy was to introduce Episcopacy to Scotland. One of the bishops ordained was Archbishop Spottiswood (he was the builder of Dairsie church). James VI was interested in Episcopacy as a method of church government but was wise enough to leave the ordinary church services alone. He did appoint Bishops e.g. John Douglas. These bishops were permanent appointments and were in charge of Synods and Assemblies. Some of the St Andrews ministers became bishops.

During the sixteenth century, the Crown appointed the ministers of the first charge and the Town Council appointed the ministers of the second charge. This continued during the seventeenth century, with the Archbishop making appointments.

The unresolved conflict of the Government with the Scottish church continued into the 17th century. King James VI, now installed in London was in a position of greater power. Matters might have remained there with the appointment of bishops, but Charles I came to the throne and was determined to interfere with the worship of the church. He introduced Archbishop Laud's new prayer book, which caused great fury among the Scots, who were by now used to spontaneous prayers. Wars ensued until the Revolution settlement of 1689, which abolished the bishops and guaranteed Presbyterian worship in Scotland. Many Scots died for their faith in what became known as the killing times. For many Scots it was a time of great piety and a very deep faith, but also of great cruelty on the part of he Government. On a local level the kirk session exercised great control over the parish, especially with regard to sexual sins.

George Gledstanes MA

George Gledstanes MA was the next minister. He was born about 1562 and a native of Dundee. He graduated at St Andrews University in 1580. He was a teacher of languages in Montrose and became Reader in 1585 in that town. He was ordained minister of St Cyrus (with Aberluthnott) in 1587 and became minister of Arbirlot in May 1592. He was on several commissions of the General Assembly, one of which was advising the King on church affairs. When the King had the Holy Trinity ministers, Black and Wallace, removed from their charge, George Gledstanes was inducted in their place on 19 July 1597. James Melville had his work cut out to have the minister accepted by the congregation because they liked Black and Wallace, but Andrew Melville thought it prudent for Gledstanes to be accepted.

When the king introduced the proposal that the church should be represented in parliament, he was supported in the assembly by Gledstanes and was appointed as one of three commissioners chosen to sit and vote in parliament in name of the ministry. He became vice-chancellor of the University of St Andrews in July 1599. He was made Bishop of Caithness on 1 November 1600, but continued as minister in St Andrews. He sat in Parliament as a bishop and was challenged by the Synod of Fife meeting in St Andrews on 3 February 1601, for doing so when he declared that he was obliged to answer "with the name of bishop put against his will, because they would not name him otherwise."

He was made a member of the Privy Council of Scotland in 1602. He was appointed one of the commissioners for the union of the Crowns. He and his brethren at the Presbytery of St Andrews renewed and subscribed to the Scots confession of Faith. He was appointed Archbishop of St Andrews on 12 October 1604, but did not tell the other ministers of St Andrews' presbytery. He declared at the presbytery meeting in 1605 that he had no superiority over the other ministers. He was asked how he could bear with the presbytery and said "hold your tongue we shall steal them off their feet."

George Gladstanes long deferred taking the title of Archbishop of St Andrews. He was obliged to vacate the castle of St Andrews but received an annual pension of 100 merks (about £13) but later the king bought the castle back and Gledstanes resided in it. Gledstanes had various disputes with Andrew Melville and also attended a conference at Hampton court in 1606.

The General Assembly, at the bidding of James VI, enacted that there should be permanent moderators for presbyteries and synods. Gledstanes was appointed president of the Presbytery of St Andrews and also the Synod of Fife. The Privy Council issued a charge to the members to obey the Act of Assembly or face the consequences, which was to be denounced as rebels. To make sure that this was carried out, four commissioners attended the synod meeting at Dysart in 1607 to induct Gledstanes as permanent Moderator. The ministers continued to resist. The ministers replied that "they would rather abide the horning (being declared outlaws) and all their fellows thereon than lose the liberty of the Kirk. The leaders were imprisoned and one was declared an outlaw.

Gledstanes meantime constituted a chapter with seven of his fellow ministers. However he fell out with King James about money and property. Gledstanes wanted the money from some estates, the customs of St Andrews and confiscated goods to be the property of the Episcopal see but James (greedy like all kings) wanted the money for the crown. Gledstanes wanted to be moderator of the General Assembly, but the king would not nominate him.

Gledstanes spent a lot of his time in Edinburgh, keeping a "splendid establishment and was surrounded by crowds of poor ministers." He customarily only preached in the forenoon, while in the afternoon, he was engaged in some pastime or lay in his bed and slept. King James placed the regulation of stipends of the clergy in the power of the bishops and distributed money among them. In 1610, just before the meeting of the assembly in June, the King gave ten thousand merks at the disposal of Gledstanes and Spottiswood.

The King called an Assembly in Glasgow on 8 June 1610. Gledstanes, acting as procurer issued invitations only from "A special note of the names of such as we desire at our King's said meeting". (inviting only those who would support him) Thus the "Angelical Assembly" of Glasgow was constituted with nobles and 133 ministers and including Gledstanes. Amongst other things the bishops were reinstated.

Gledstanes was consecrated a bishop along with other bishops in 1611. (He was appointed a bishop before being consecrated.) He was Chancellor of St Andrews University from 1604 to 1615 and revived the divinity teaching there.

Gledstanes was not well treated financially by the king, who did not make proper provision for the bishops. Gledstanes was so poor that he said that in the event of his death "in what case should I leave my children if God should visit me, He knows."

He died on 2 May 1615 of "a loathsome disease " and was buried immediately (illegally) in Holy Trinity church, but there was a big funeral a month later paid by King James. This funeral took place on 7 June 1615 on a windy stormy day. Four men carried the coffin when the canopy of black velvet over the empty coffin blew away, exposing the coffin. Bishop William Cowper gave his funeral sermon.

A contemporary reference was that "he was a competent portion of pedantry, was abundantly vainglorious and at the same time possessed all the obsequiousness which is required in one who is to be raised to the prelacy. "

However Lyon in his history of St Andrews gives a more kindly view of Gledstanes. "Mr George Gladstanes departed this life, a man of good learning, ready utterance and good invention, but also of an easy nature and induced by those he trusted to do anything hurtful together, especially in leasing the tithes to his benefice for many ages to come. He was esteemed by this means that he should purchase the love and friendship of men whereas there is no sure friend but that which is joined by respect and to the preventing of this nothing conduceth more than a wise and prudent administration of church rents wherewith they are entrusted." Another comment was made "he accepted the Episcopal office upon good warrant." Spottiswood said, "he was a man of good learning, ready utterance and great invention, but too easy a nature."

During his ministry, Gledstanes gave St Andrews privileges, shore dues and the free use of the links.

One wonders how much of his time he gave to the congregation of Holy Trinity.

Other events in early 1600's.

In 1610, The Crown arranged for bishops to be recognised as permanent Presidents of presbytery.

In 1612, Holy Trinity church bought the Authorised version of the Bible for ten shillings and six pence. It is still in the church.

James VI and I received an address of welcome in Latin by the University Rector, Mr Bruce during his visit on 11 July 1617 in the porch.

The five articles of Perth

During 1618 the **five articles of Perth** were proclaimed. Worship was to be "decent and comlie". The five articles were:

1- The Sacrament of the body and blood of Christ was to be received kneeling.

2- Communion might be administered to the sick privately.

3- Baptism might be administered in private houses when necessary.

4- Children of 8 years old should be presented for confirmation.

5- Christmas, Easter, The Resurrection, Ascension Day and the sending of the Holy Ghost were to be commemorated. Weekly worship was instituted.

The five articles were not well received by the people of Scotland.

Alexander Gladstanes MA DD

Alexander Gladstanes MA DD (1612-1638), the son of George Gledstanes was presented by James VI to be his successor to the charge. He graduated MA of St Andrews in 1608 and also obtained the degree of DD in 1619. He was presented and admitted to the First Charge of Holy Trinity on 6 April 1612. He was deposed on 4 December 1638 for drunkenness and other crimes, mainly doctrinal e.g. Arminianism. While this is a precise theological term relating to the teaching of the Dutch theologian Arminius, it became a catch-all term for heresy if you wanted rid of someone for another reason. There is no evidence now to substantiate this but the Kirk Session records are missing for 1600-1638. The petition of his daughter says "He carried himself faithfully and loyally for his Majesty's interest and did advance the same as far as did lay on his power; for which he was by those who prevailed in power for the time not only most maliciously thrust from his charge but also in the year 1638 was forced to take exile upon him and went into England." Was he really an incompetent minister or was his support for Charles I, not accepted by the other ministers at this time? To support this views that the issue was support for Episcopalian doctrine. Lyon in his History of St Andrews said that Alexander Gladstanes dismissal was "for reading the liturgy, preaching anti-Calvinism and protesting against the Covenant."

Alexander Gladstanes preached at the General Assembly held in at St Andrews in November 1617 re the changed liturgy. It was agreed that home Communion for the sick be given and that clergy should give Communion out of his or her own hands.

He went to live in England and was in great poverty "having left behind his wife, family and small children." He died in 1641. His daughter petitioned Charles II in 1662 and was awarded £100 sterling.

Joshua Durie MA

Joshua Durie MA was translated from Logie and was admitted to the Second Charge of Holy Trinity on 22 October 1606. He was translated to Inverkeilor on 6 October 1613.

David Barclay DD

David Barclay DD came from Touch near Stirling. He was minister of Dailly in 1590, Maybole 1599, and Dumfries 1601 and was minister of Kilwinning in 1605. He was admitted to the Second Charge of Holy Trinity in 1614. He received a DD of St Andrews in 1616. The Court of High Commission suspended him for an unknown offence on 21 April 1620. He was admitted as minister of Dairsie in October 1630. He died on 12 January 1655.

John Douglas MA DD

John Douglas MA DD was minister of the Second Charge of Holy Trinity He was minister of Holy Trinity from 1621 to 1624. He was translated to Crail in 1624. He died preaching in the church pulpit.

George Dewar MA

George Dewar MA was minister of the Second Charge of Holy Trinity from 1624 to 1626. He was then translated to Anstruther.

Samuel Rutherford

In 1639 the famous minister Samuel Rutherford preached in Holy Trinity. A commentator said, "he was a small fair man who showed the love of Christ"

He was minister of Anworth and was eventually banished to Aberdeen for non-conformity but eventually became Professor of Divinity at St Andrews University and Rector of St Mary's College. He wrote Lex Rex and other books.

Chapter 4
The reign of Charles I (1625-1649)
Introduction

James VI had managed to introduce Episcopacy, but otherwise he left the church alone. The majority of the members were not greatly worried about the changes, but Charles I was about to introduce changes that would affect services. He was interested in having a uniform church both in Scotland and England.

In 1637, Charles I introduced a Revised Prayer Book to Scotland on his own initiative. The bishops approved it, but not Parliament or the rest of the church. Extemporary prayer was forbidden. On its introduction to St Giles in Edinburgh, there was a riot with a woman named Jenny Geddes throwing her stool at the Bishop taking the service saying "Daur thou say mass at my lug". In Brechin, there was complete acquiescence, because the bishop laid two loaded pistols on the lectern before starting the service. John Spottiswood was Archbishop at the time.

The National Covenant was signed in Greyfriars churchyard in 1638. Charles I agreed to call a General Assembly, which was the first for 20 years and it met in 1638. The assembly abolished the bishops. The bishops fled to England. The new Prayer Book was declared unlawful. The General Assembly also declared the Five Articles of Perth null and void. The Westminster confession was written and adopted in 1643 and this is still the standard creed of the Church of Scotland.

George Wishart MA, DD

George Wishart MA, DD was Minister of the second charge 1626-1637. He was born in 1599 and studied at Edinburgh and graduated from St Andrews in 1613. He became Minister of Monifieth in 1624. He moved to the Second Charge of Holy Trinity, St Andrews on 18 April 1626. When the Presbyterians gained ascendancy, he fled to England along with Archbishop Spottiswood and was deposed for deserting his charge. In 1639 he was appointed to All Saints,

Newcastle. In 1640 he was presented at St Nicholas, Newcastle. When Leslie and the Scots army took Newcastle in 1644, Wishart was taken prisoner on the charge of corresponding with Royalists. He was imprisoned in the thief's hole in Edinburgh. In 1645, the Estates of Parliament agreed to support his wife and five children. After 7 months in prison, Wishart was liberated when the Marquis of Montrose arrived in Edinburgh after his victory at Kilsyth on 15th August 1645. Wishart joined the Royal Army at Bothwell and was appointed private chaplain to the Marquis of Montrose. He accompanied the Marquis in his campaigns at home and abroad. He wrote a biography of Montrose's campaigns. Montrose was tried in absentia in 1649. Wishart's book was brought in evidence against Montrose. Montrose was (in absentia) sentenced to be hanged with Wishart's book round his neck. Montrose was captured in 1650 and the sentence carried out on 21st May 1650. After the fall of Montrose, Wishart became chaplain to a Scottish regiment of the Prince of Orange and minister at Scheidam. After the Restoration of Charles II Wishart was appointed rector of Newcastle. When Montrose's body parts were buried in St Giles Cathedral, a stained glass window bearing the arms of Montrose's supporters including those of Dr George Wishart was inserted. Dr Wishart became Bishop of Edinburgh in 1662. He died on 25th July 1671 and his epitaph in Latin can be seen on a mural in the Church of Holyrood House.

It would appear that most of the Holy Trinity ministers did not object to episcopacy, and were willing to become Bishops if they were chosen. The National Covenant of 1638 was not subscribed to in St Andrews. There were other important documents found at this time including Lauds Liturgy, which was read in St Andrews in 1637, apparently without riots. The Westminster Assembly and Standards and the Shorter Catechism, was approved by Parliament in 1649, but not considered in the Revolution Settlement of 1690.

Robert Blair MA

Robert Blair MA was born at Irvine in 1593. He was educated at the University of Glasgow and licensed in 1616. He was appointed Professor of Philosophy in that institution. He resigned when he could not support his Principal, Dr John Cameron, and James Law, Archbishop of Glasgow over their enthusiasm for Episcopacy. Robert Blair was opposed to them in his beliefs about Episcopacy, and this "rendered his life uneasy" so he was required to seek a position elsewhere. He was ordained in 1623, after consulting Bishop Knox, who advised him to be ordained as a Presbyter in a neighbouring presbytery. He became minister of Bangor but disagreed with the Bishop of Down over Episcopacy. He was deposed by Bishop Echlim in 1631, but was re-ordained through the intervention of Archbishop Usher and Charles I. Robert Blair had sent a petition to Charles 1, who wrote in the margin "indulge these men for they are Scotsmen." Bishop Echlim deposed him and a neighbour, Mr John Livingstone, again in November 1634, and ordered him to be apprehended. He escaped to Scotland and became minister of Ayr in 1638. By order of the Privy Council he was admitted to the first charge of Holy Trinity in 1639.

Robert Blair was away from Holy Trinity in much of the time during his first few years there. Blair went away with the army, which invaded England in 1640, as a chaplain. He was away again with the army in 1642 in Ireland.

Robert Blair was an enthusiastic supporter of the Solemn League and Covenant of 1643 (it was an agreement which confirmed Presbyterianism in Scotland and also in England, but the English side of the agreement was never likely to be fulfilled). When the General Assembly accepted the amended Covenant, Blair said "When the draught thereof, at last agreed unto, was read in an open audience of the whole Assembly our smoking desires for a more strict union and uniformity of religion between both the nations did break forth into a vehement flame: for it was so unanimously and heartily embraced (so sincere was the Church of Scotland in this grand affair) and with such a torrent of most affectionate expressions as none but eye and ear witnesses can conceive" (Blair was present).

In July 1644, Robert Blair was present at the battle of Marston Moor. It was a decisive battle. He then went home to St Andrews.

In 1645, the Parliament and the Commission of Assembly met at Perth. Robert Blair preached to them. He then met the army at Forgandenny. The army fought two battles, but was then defeated by Montrose's army at Philiphaugh.

When Lord President Spottiswood was sent to the scaffold in 1645 after the Battle of Philiphaugh, Robert Blair attended him and the other condemned men.

In 1646, the Parliament and the Commission of Assembly met at St Andrews.

Robert Blair was Moderator of the General Assembly of 1646.

He was ordered to go as a Commissioner to see Charles I at Newcastle to try to persuade the King from his Episcopalian views. He was unable to shake the king's Episcopalian views and Charles, who appointed him King's chaplain for Scotland in 1646 in place of Alexander Henderson, who had died, favoured his conciliatory tone.

He was sent along with Mr David Dickson and James Guthrie to negotiate with Oliver Cromwell in 1648. He disliked Cromwell and distrusted his extreme Puritan views but was appointed by Cromwell to the General Assembly of 1648. He asked Cromwell to answer three questions, firstly about monarchial government, secondly about toleration of different opinions and thirdly about the government of the church. Cromwell evaded the questions.

Mr Dickson, rubbing his elbow said that he was very glad to hear Oliver Cromwell speak as he did. Mr Blair replied, asking if Mr Dickson believed Cromwell. Mr Blair said that if Mr Dickson knew Cromwell as he did you would not believe a word he said. Mr Blair said that Cromwell was an egregious dissembler and a great liar. Mr Blair said, "Away with Cromwell he is a greeting devil."

In 1651, Mr Blair was removed to Musselburgh and Kirkcaldy. In 1652, Mr Blair was so disenhearted with the General Assembly that he returned to St

Andrews. In 1654, Cromwell summoned him to London. But he excused himself due to ill health.

When Mr Blair was in London, there was a division of the church into Resolutioners and Protesters. The Resolutioners were the Royalists along with others who supported King Charles II, although suspicious of his motives. The Protestors were extreme Presbyterians, who believed the defeat at Dunbar in 1650 was due to God's disapproval of the attachment of the Army to the King. The two groups held rival General Assemblies in 1653. Mr Blair and Mr Durham (minister of Glasgow) tried hard to reconcile the differences, but they were unable to reach agreement.

Mr Blair preached sermons in Holy Trinity from the following texts:
1 November 1649 from John 15; 6.
18 November 1649 from John 15:12
4 November 1649 from Psalm 45: and 1 John 1
6 November 1649 from John 15:8
January 1651 from Isaiah 4:4.
1661 1 Peter 3:13.

Some other stories about Robert Blair

It was stated that in the time of the Commonwealth, Mr Blair was called before the English counsel who intended to take his position and pension as King's chaplain. Mr Blair made a wise appearance before them, so that when he was removed they said "it is as well that this man is a minister for if this man were not a minister he might vex us all with his great wisdom and policy. Therefore let us not take his pension from him but let him keep it." And so they dismissed him with great respect. He was reckoned one of the wisest men of the Nation. [1]

When Mr Blair had gone to the Court, he procured the king's letter to Deputy Stafford. Stafford stormed and raged at it and started cursing and

---

[1] (Analecta 3 Page 91)

swearing before Mr Blair. Mr Blair said, "Blessed be the name of the Lord" at which Deputy Stafford turned silent and ever after became Mr Blair's friend.

Robert Blair's son, Mr David Blair said that his father was once riding with the famous Mr David Dickson (Professor of Divinity New College Edinburgh) and he was going to tell Mr Dickson some remarkable thing and immediately his horse fell with him, and had almost killed him or did him considerable damage. However he was safe. When he mounted again Mr Dickson desired him to proceed with what he was saying, but Mr Blair said "No more must be said about that matter! I have met with enough at this time to stop me: [2] Pride is very ready to get in upon us: and it may be what I have met with is a reproof".

Mr. Wodrow made the comment "So tender was this holy man."

Mr Wodrow senior (as a student) complained of his slavish fear that he feared might hinder him from speaking in public and preaching. "Be not discouraged, Jacob" said Mr Blair, for now I have been fifty three years in the ministry and to this day when I am to preach, the sound of the third bell gives a knell to my heart and sets me almost a trembling." (The third bell was rung at the start of the sermon.)

Mr Wodrow senior also said that when he was a young man, he went to St Andrews to hear Mr Blair; but Mr Blair would have him hear Mr Rutherford and not himself; but Mr Wodrow heard Mr Blair lecture on Sunday night in his own house and Mr Wodrow said "but how divinely did he speak as one in Heaven on that exercise." Mr Blair said to Mr Wodrow that how it had been very well with him that day. [3] Mr Blair said that when he had done with his study, he had his sermon but his work was just beginning. After the sermon was done, he spent much time in prayer so that God would remove the material that belonged to Mr Blair and remove it from Mr Blair's eyes during delivery of the sermon.

Mr Blair was hardly ever at a loss whether preaching or in prayer; he was an excellent orator and he was never confused as to his allegiance to Christ.

---

[2] (Analecta 2 Page 91)
[3] (Analecta 3 Page 91)

One providential story related to Mr Blair was crossing a river or loch, which he did not know, when he saw a cow drinking at a different place. Mr Blair followed the cow and went across the water at another place. When he asked a man about what would have happened if he had crossed the water at the original place, the man replied "if you had crossed the water there you would have been lost."

Mr Blair desired to meet with Mr Rutherford (Minister of Anworth) and Marion McNaught and was riding his horse, when he came to a junction of paths. He did not know which way to take so he let his horse take whatever way the horse wanted to go and the horse went straight to Kirkcudbright to Marion McNaught's house, where he found Mr Rutherford and if he had gone to Anworth, he would not have met either of them.

A strange story about a trainee minister

A youth applied to the Presbytery of St Andrews to be admitted to trials for being ordained as a minister. Being very unfit to prepare for these trials, he found that the text appointed by the brethren to be beyond his capacity. One day, when he was walking dejectedly to a place remote from St Andrews, he was accosted by a stranger dressed as a minister. When he told this minister his story, he was supplied by an excellent sermon on the text. The stranger made him promise to give future service when required and insisted that the bargain be sealed with the young man's blood. Rev Blair sensed the work of the Devil and examined the young man and discovered the truth. The Presbytery in great alarm appointed the next day for a second prayer meeting in a quiet church. Rev Robert Blair prayed last and in the time of his prayer there came a violent rushing of wind upon the church so great that they thought that the church would have fallen down about their ears and then the youth's paper and covenant falls down from he roof of the church among the ministers. [4]

If you discount Wodrow's infatuation with the devil it is a plausible story. The only changes to make it credible are to make the minister a real minister

---

[4] (From Analecta 1 102-104 –the story came from Mr John Glasford minister of Stracathro)

giving the young man the sermon as he felt sorry for him, discounting the signing in blood and the real alarm of the presbytery at finding the student had not conducted his trials honestly. Mr Blair seemed to have been a very acute minister.

Stories about Mr. Blair and the church

Mr. Moiré heard this from Mr. Vilant who was told it by Robert Blair. There was a gentleman, who lived within a mile or two of St Andrews, who was of very good qualifications of great sense and bookish and used to take up all the differences among his neighbours (i.e. settled their quarrels). But he was frequently overtaken with drink when he came to St Andrews. Mr. Blair had no acquaintance with him at all and did not so much know him face to face. However he resolved to go out and pay him a visit and bear himself upon him as well as he could and reprove him for drinking. Accordingly one afternoon he took his horse and rode out to give him a visit. When he came near his house, at a little burn, he met with the gentleman and stopped his horse to allow the horse to drink. Mr. Blair asked him "How far is it to the gentleman's house"? The gentleman told him so far and asked if he was going there and told him he was the gentleman. The gentleman's horse was drinking and Mr. Blair's horse would not drink. After the gentleman offered to go back with him (knowing Mr. Blair, though Mr. Blair did not know him) Mr. Blair said that he would say nothing he wanted to in that place: and began to talk, starting with his horse refusing to drink when he had no need of it and Mr. Blair told the gentleman what a good character he had, except for his drinking and laid out the evil of excessive drinking. But the gentleman took his advice badly and spurred his horse and rode off without a farewell. Mr. Blair resolved to try again and a month later went out one day to see him. When he came to the same place by the burn as before, he saw a horse eating by the waterside with a saddle and nobody with it. When he rode in the water, he saw a man lying face down in the water He first thought it was someone lying down to drink but quickly saw that the man was dead. He pulled the man out and saw that it was the same gentleman that he spoke with a month previously. The man went into St Andrews, became drunk and when the horse was drinking the water, the man fell off.

Some ministers asked Mr. Blair what he thought and Mr. Blair replied "in the place where he rejected the counsel of God, the Lord slew him.

Mr. Warner (Balmacllelan) and John Welsh (Irongray) visited Robert Blair who was then at Aberdour in 1664. Mr. Blair fell to encourage them under the sad prospect they had and said "You are but young men and the Lord will gloriously revive his work now buried. I am an old man and it will be much if I see it. But Mr. Warner shall see it. (Mr. Warner saw the Revolution). [5]

Mr. Blair had been a while at St Andrews and observed many people leaving the church a little before pronouncing the blessing. After taking some pains to reform them from this custom, one day after prayer he told them he had one word to speak to them after Psalms and desired them to stay. When the Psalms were done, he said "Now the prettiest man and woman among you now all run first and fastest from the blessing". This had it seems more influence on them than all his former pains and they refrained afterwards from leaving the church early. [6]

Mr. Robert Blair, when speaking of Elihu in Job's affair called him "God's moderator" His talent was in holding them out of the majesty and excellency of God and several times to say "O Our God is a great God" O that his enemies knew how great a God he is. [7]

About 1654, Mr. Blair rose at 5 a.m. on a day set apart for private prayer. His wife came in at breakfast, dinner and night but got no answer. She was uneasy and said to him that if he did not speak she would force her way in. When Mr. Blair opened the door she said that his health was in hazard and that he was neglecting his body. Mr. Blair said that he was wrestling for the Church of Scotland and had got enemies but the Prince of Orange (who was at that time an infant) would be the church's deliverer. [8]

---

[5] (Analecta 1 Page 58)

[6] (Analecta 1 Page 66)

[7] (Analecta 1 Page 146)

The story of the gentleman from London

He came to St Andrews in the forenoon and heard the majesty and stateliness of God laid out, as he never had heard before. In the afternoon, after a sermon from Mr. Rutherford (Anworth) his heart was melted with "the loveliness of Christ "and next day in Glasgow he heard a little old man, Mr. Dickinson, who told him with all his heart "Those were their three talents." It was observed of Mr. Blair that he was seldom in his preaching lost for words and was never confused.

Mr. Rutherford was extremely and almost excessively charitable. He was naturally hot and fiery. In the time of the differences between the Resolutioners and Protestors at a Communion at St Andrews, Mr. Rutherford refused to serve at a table where Mrs. Blair and Mr. Wood (Professor of Divinity St Mary's College) sat; despite they were pleading with him to serve them. At length Mr. Blair was forced to serve the table himself. When Mr. Blair began, he was exceedingly disheartened with Mr. Rutherford's behaviour and began to speak "We have water in our wine while here. O to be above where there will be no mistakes." Yet Mr. Rutherford was to preach in the afternoon after the tables: and did so but was remarkably deserted. Some people that came to Communion from Galloway remarked on it and lamented over the divisions. Mr. Rutherford was very humble and would never call Mr. Blair "Brother" but called him "Sir". [9]

Despite all this work, Robert Blair was removed from Holy Trinity and St Andrews in September 1661 after the restoration of Charles II to the throne. The reason was that Blair was an out spoken critic of Archbishop Sharp. Sharp prohibited Blair from coming within 20 miles of St Andrews. Mr Blair commenced his exile in Edinburgh, Inveresk (January 1662) and Kirkcaldy and finally spent the rest of his life at Couston Castle at Aberdour in Fife.

Two months before Robert Blair's death, he was in company with Mr Alexander Dunlop and Mr Robert Cunningham. They were talking about the church. Mr Robert Blair then fell silent and continued in a deep muse for three-

---

[8] (Analecta page 331 1719)

[9] (Analecta page 146)

quarters of an hour. When his meditation was over he said to them "Do you know what I have been thinking about? It is very strange to me and will be to you. The Church of Scotland will never be right until the Prince of Orange will be King of Great Britain".

When Mr Blair was dying his granddaughter was very ill and Mr Blair asked that she be brought to him. He laid one hand on her sore and lifting his eyes upwards said, "my God shall heal my child." And after that although the physicians had given up on her she was perfectly whole.

Robert Blair wrote "A Commentary on Proverbs " (1666).

Robert Blair died on 27 August 1667. He was buried in the nearby Kirkyard of Aberdour. His gravestone records his life in Latin "The body of D Robert Blair SS, Most faithful evangelist among the St Andreans, died August 27 1667 His age 73."

As a final **tribute** to Mr Blair's life these are the words of Mr William Vilant (Minister Ferry Port on Craig) "Scarcely did he know of a more rare conjunction of these three things, more eminently shining in any one minister, then Mr Blair, viz. eminent piety, prudence and learning and a most peaceable calm temper of spirit."

When Robert Blair died Archbishop Sharp said "He was the man with the most powerful gift of prayer ever he knew." [10]

Andrew Honeyman MA

Andrew Honeyman MA was born in 1619. He was minister of Ferry Port on Craig and was inducted into the Second charge in 1642. He ministered until 1662 and then he was translated minister of the first charge from 2 October 1662 to 1664. He was made Bishop of Orkney on 11 April 1664.

Mr Honeyman preached sermons in Holy Trinity from the following texts:

---

[10] (Analecta Page 300)

Sunday 15 November 1649 from Colossians 3:13:

Saturday 3 November 1649: Luke 3:4.

Mr. Blair, Mr. Wood (Professor Glasgow University) Mr. Rutherford (Anworth) and Mr. Honeyman (St Andrews)

Mr. Rutherford and Mr. Wood differed in their views on the Public Resolutions, yet Mr. Rutherford had great esteem for Mr. Wood and respected his honesty. After a meeting about the subject Mr. Rutherford spoke and Mr. Wood did not meddle with him but Mr. Rutherford spoke sharply against Mr. Honeyman though Mr. Honeyman spoke and agreed with Mr. Wood. Mr. Blair said to Mr. Rutherford "Why are you so partial?" Mr. Blair said "Why do you let Mr. Wood win away without ever contradicting him when you fall upon poor Mr. Honeyman with such severity". Mr. Rutherford said "I know Mr. Wood is very wrong in that particular point: but he is an honest man and will prove to be an honest man but your colleague Mr. Honeyman is a knave and will prove a knave." (He took a bishopric in 1664)

Mr. James Wood (St Mary's College) preached the gospel and practical truths and meddled little with public affairs. Mr. Honeyman preached vehemently on all public debates. One day Mr. Honeyman in his sermon said that there was a minister in St Andrews who was too silent and did not act his part in giving faithful warning about the behaviour of the people. Mr. Wood met Mr. Honeyman and was calm and good tempered but Mr. Honeyman railed at him and stood by on what he said. [11]

Mr. Honeyman went to Edinburgh and informed the King's advocate against Mr. Blair. Letters came calling Mr. Blair before the Privy Council. Mr. Blair denied the facts inferred. Mr. Honeyman adhered to the persecution of Mr. Blair but failed in carrying it out.

When Mr. Honeyman was minister, he was asked by the Presbytery of St Andrews in 1660 to write a testimony against Episcopacy and the presbytery approved this. Mr. Hutcheon and Mr. Douglas reviewed it and admired it.   But

---

[11] (Analecta page 325 1715)

when James Sharp came to St Andrews, Honeyman was made Dean but even then he was not satisfied. When this was related to James Sharp, Sharp said "I know how to stop his mouth by a bishopric". He was consecrated bishop of Orkney in 1664.

As an example of the business of the Kirk Session at that time, Mr Honeyman and his colleague Mr Robert Blair had some difficulty with one of the local nobility, as shown in the following story.

On 15 November 1643. Mr. Robert Blair declared that while he and his colleague, Mr. Andrew Honeyman, with the Gudeman of Kemback, and James Wood, Baillie of St. Andrews, being sent by the Session of St. Andrews to Sir James Lundie, inhabitant in the town, to desire him to keep the diets of the public worship of God, as he did not attend the public worship in the last year. He was so far from promising amendment, that he behaved himself rudely toward the said Mr. Robert Blair and when his hat was in his hand, he put it on his head, and gave him a direct lie. The Presbytery ordained him to be summoned to come before them the next day.

On 7 February 1643, Mr. Andrew Honeyman, being examined, declared, that the said Sir James, being accused for staying so long from the public worship of God in the Kirk, he promised no amendment, but behaved himself rudely toward Mr. Robert Blair, with his hat on his head when Mr. Robert's hat was in his hand, and said, *If ye will say that, Sir, I will say, ye lie; or if any in Scotland will say it, I will say he lies.' Thereupon Sir James was summoned and directed to "keep the kirk".[12]

When Mr Honeyman was in Edinburgh in 1668, he sat in a carriage with Archbishop Sharp. An assassin named James Mitchell fired at the Archbishop but struck Honeyman on the wrist and so shattered the bone that it was ultimately the cause of his death. Honeyman wrote an answer to "Naphthali" (Sir James Bruce) in two parts in 1668 and 1669. His last sermon was on 18 August 1675. He died on 21 February 1676 and was buried in St Magnus Cathedral, Kirkwall.

---

[12] (Analecta page 325 1715)

What is our verdict on the unfortunate Mr Honeyman? He was clearly ambitious and this did not go down too well with his colleague Mr Blair. He also appeared to have some malice towards Mr Blair and possibly he favoured the solution of having bishops in the church. But he met a dreadful end, being ill for so long after the shooting.

Renovations.

The church was renovated in 1642.

New church Cameron

In 1645, a new church and parish was created at Cameron. This reduced the parish of Holy Trinity but also decreased the income by assigning most of the vicarage teinds to Cameron.

Oliver Cromwell's government (1651-1660)

General Monck, who occupied the country, oversaw the government in Scotland. The Magistrates of St Andrews feared for the safety of their valuables, including plate and so sent these articles to Dundee for safety. But General Monck and his soldiers besieged and sacked the city and the soldiers looted all the plate.

During the revolution under Oliver Cromwell, the General Assembly of the church was banned in 1653, but Cromwell allowed religious toleration. The

General Assembly did not meet again until 1690. The two ministers Robert Blair and Andrew Honeyman ministered during the Commonwealth. The sermons of the two ministers for 4 July 1658 are in the National Assembly. Communion was not celebrated for several years between 1653 and 1658.

During the Commonwealth, Mr. Blair along with Mr. Durham (Glasgow) wanted to promote a union between the two church parties, Resolutioners and Protesters, in order to present a united front to negotiate with the government. The Resolutioners wanted to have a delegate to Cromwell to present their case and suggested James Sharp. Mr. Blair was unfavourable to the suggestion (Mr. Blair saw what Sharp was like). The Protesters sent their own delegate James Simpson of Airth. Cromwell appointed a Council of 12 members to listen to the delegates. Cromwell said that he would listen to them at a more convenient time and go home and live at peace.

Chapter 5

Episcopacy reintroduced

However Episcopacy was reintroduced under Charles II in 1661 and this was not changed until the settlement of 1689. However Charles II allowed the Kirk Sessions, Presbyteries and Synods to convene and allowed Presbyterian worship without the prayer book. New bishops were ordained in 1661 and their unpopularity led to 320 of the ministers removing themselves from the churches and holding meetings in the countryside, where they were hunted by Government troops. Neither of the Holy Trinity ministers left the church voluntarily. However Archbishop Sharp hated Robert Blair and had him removed to Dalgety. Ministers had to seek confirmation from the bishop and the patron, but this did not appear to deter some of the Holy Trinity ministers.

Worship made use of the Lord's Prayer, although even this was frowned upon by the extreme Presbyterians. There was a call for shorter sermons but on the whole there was little difference between Presbyterian and Episcopalian worship at this time.

It would appear that some members were unhappy about the situation as the men who murdered Archbishop Sharp came from the locality of St Andrews. There were laws against the meetings to hold religious services in the countryside, and the people who were holding or attending these services could be killed without trial if they were caught. Not for anything was the period from 1680-1688 called the killing times.

Conventicles.

Conventicles were open-air services held by banned ministers. Often when a minister was banned for his opposition to Episcopacy, he and his congregation met wherever they could and this included barns and fields. The only banned minister of St Andrews was Robert Blair and he did not hold conventicles, as he was probably too old at the time. Nevertheless conventicles were held in the vicinity of St Andrews led by banned ministers from other places. A conventicle was held at Anstruther in May 1668 with Michael Bruce preaching. Another example was the conventicle held at Dura, between St Andrews and Cupar in 1674 where a banned minister, Rev John Welsh of Kilpatrick Irongray presided. 8000 people attended and obviously some of these came from St Andrews parish. The dragoons heard about the conventicle but the congregation heard about the dragoons, so all escaped.

Another conventicle was held at Kinkell in 1674, where Rev Sir John Blackadder of Troqueer preached. Archbishop Sharp heard about the conventicle, so he ordered the Provost of St Andrews to call out the militia. The Provost replied that they were already there listening to the preacher. The Archbishop was much dampened (disappointed) when he heard this.

Mr. Alexander Hamilton of Kinkell, who was previously an elder of Holy Trinity and who had not attended Holy Trinity church for a year and had attended conventicles instead, probably had arranged the conventicles at Kinkell.

Rev Sir John Blackadder also preached at Moonzie (near Cupar) on an unknown date.

There also was a conventicle held at Falkland in 1675. Allan Cameron, merchant in Falkland, his wife Margaret Paterson, his son Richard Cameron MA and Michael Cameron attended. Richard Gillespie an irregular preacher was taken at a Conventicle at Falkland and sent to the Bass Rock.

A banned ex-minister of Cupar, Thomas Arnot, held further conventicles. Troops were quartered in Cupar in 1676. Some people attending conventicles were arrested and escaped from the Cupar Tolbooth in 1677.

There is very little information on the many Conventicles held in the vicinity of St Andrews. Yet a large number of the population were sympathetic to the Covenanters, as it proved impossible to apprehend the murderers of Archbishop Sharp.

Alexander Young

Alexander Young, who was born in Aberdeen, was minister of Cramond. He was minister of the first charge of Holy Trinity from 28 September 1665 until 1671. He was consecrated Bishop of Edinburgh on 14 July 1672 and became Bishop of Ross in 1679. He suffered from an ailment. In 1684, he went to France and died a few weeks later.

Andrew Bruce

Andrew Bruce, (1673-1679) was presented to the church by Archbishop James Sharp and ordained on 21 January 1673. He was Professor of Divinity at New College in addition to being minister of the First Charge of Holy Trinity.

During his ministry at Holy Trinity, the transept, where the tomb of Archbishop Sharp was later placed, was constructed. Andrew Bruce was consecrated bishop of Dunkeld 28 October 1679. He was deprived of the Bishopric in 1686 for disapproving of certain newly created laws. Two years later in 1688, he was made Bishop of Orkney but only held the position for a few months because of the Glorious Revolution brought an end to episcopacy. He died in March 1700.

William Moore MA DD

The Town Council and the heritors elected William Moore MA DD, as the next minister. He was admitted minister of Dunino on 1 November 1663 and translated to the Second Charge of Holy Trinity on 9 July 1664 and he was admitted to that charge on 15 July 1664. He was a DD of St Andrews in 1672.

The Kirk Session and heritors elected him to the First Charge of Holy Trinity and he was translated and admitted on 21 October 1680, but he died on

26 March 1684. He was about 65 years old. He left £100 for the poor and his library to St Salvator's College.

Robert Honeyman MA DD

Robert Honeyman MA DD, was minister of the second charge of Holy Trinity between 1681 and 1686. He was born in 1624 and graduated at St Andrews University. He was Regent of St Leonard's College, St Andrews and was successively minister of Newburn then Dysart and then Cupar. He was introduced into the Second Charge of Holy Trinity on 10 February 1681, inducted on 7 July 1681 and died in March 1686.

Archbishop James Sharp

One minister who abandoned Presbyterianism was James Sharp.

Sharp was born on 4 May 1618 at Banff Castle and attended Aberdeen University, where he graduated MA. He went to England and returned to Scotland and became a Professor of Philosophy at St Salvator's College. He became minister of Crail. He plotted with General Monck for the return of Charles II to the throne. Sharp also met Charles II, but their conversations were secret so it is not known what was said. Sharp must have known what the King's views were. King Charles II was restored to the throne in 1660 and in 1661, the Privy Council restored Episcopacy, forbade the meeting of clerical courts and stated that non–conformists should be imprisoned. In December 1662 James Sharp became Archbishop of St Andrews. He preached his introductory sermon in Holy Trinity on 17 April 1662 and his sermon came from 1 Corinthians 2:2 "I am determined not to know anything among you save Jesus Christ and him crucified."

One story was that the Public Resolutioners (one of the ministerial parties) sent James Sharp to London. When he was made Archbishop, the ministers promised to pay his charges and gave him twenty shillings sterling. Those that joined with him paid their quota but those who did not agree with episcopacy refused to pay. He gave a bill to the Clerk Register to oblige them to pay him. The Clerk Register delayed bringing in the bill. At last pressed by Archbishop Sharp, it came in and the Register said openly in Court "This man is worse than Judas, who when he betrayed his master gave back his thirty pieces but this man not only betrays his constituents but will force them to pay for so doing."

There are many stories about Archbishop Sharp, but we record only two of them. They both ascribe supernatural powers to the Archbishop and in particular that he was in league with the devil. The stories are recorded not because they can be taken at face value, but to show what people thought of him.

The first of the two stories about Archbishop Sharp. When the Archbishop was presiding in the Privy Council he had Jane Douglas brought before the Council accusing her of witchcraft. She vindicated herself of the accusation, declaring that she knew very well who were witches, yet she was not one herself for she was trying to discover the witches' plots and to countermine them. The Archbishop said that she might be sent to the plantations in the West Indies. She said one word to the bishop "My Lord who was with you in your closet on Saturday night between midnight and one o'clock." The Bishop turned pale and promised that she should not be sent to America. (The storyteller implied that James Sharp met the Devil, but it is more likely that it was some person that James Sharp did not wish the public to know that he was having negotiations.)

The second story about Archbishop Sharp. Sharp was in Edinburgh as a member of the Privy Council and was busy prosecuting some men who had taken part in the Pentland Rising. He needed a paper, which was in his cabinet in St Andrews. He dispatched his footman to bring it to him and gave the footman directions and the key to the cabinet. The footman left at 10 o'clock and was in St Andrews at 4 o'clock, having run very fast. When he arrived he saw the Archbishop sitting at a table near the window as if he had been reading and writing. The footman was surprised but called out "Well done my Lord well ridden indeed. I saw you in Edinburgh at 10 o'clock and yet you are here before me. The Archbishop looked at him with a sour face but did not say anything. The footman ran downstairs and told the secretary that the Archbishop had come home. He did not believe the footman but both went up and saw the Archbishop standing at the stair head staring at them with an angry look. When the footman went into the closet there was no–one there so he opened the cabinet took the paper and went back to Edinburgh. Next morning he met the Archbishop gave him the paper and told his story. The Archbishop then swore him to secrecy.

Political problems

Meantime another former Covenanter, John Middleton was appointed King's commissioner for Scotland. He was a nasty violent man and a heavy drinker. He managed to have new laws passed by Parliament including MIddleton's Act on 11 June 1662, where ministers ordained after 1649 and who was holding appointments from congregations or Presbyteries had to be presented by the patron and the appointment ratified by the bishop. About 320 of the clergy were outed from their parishes for disobeying the Act. Other Acts of Parliament included the "Bishops drag net" which imposed heavy fines on those who did not attend church "to hear the curates" and the Scots mile Act which forbade outed ministers from living within twenty miles of their former church and within fifteen miles of Edinburgh. Hence the former minister of Holy Trinity, Robert Blair had to live in Dalgety.

When the parliament broke up in 1663, it was not recalled, leaving the running of the country to the Privy Council. King Charles II was persuaded by James Sharp to bring back the obsolete Court of High Commission. James Sharp was appointed President of the Court, which had wide ranging, powers and James Sharp used these powers in a tyrannous fashion. There was an incident where some soldiers were attempting to ill-treat an old man by torturing him with a branding iron. The soldiers were killed and this led to a full-scale rebellion ending in the Battle of Rullion Green in 1666.

After the Battle of Rullion Green, James Sharp was most vociferous in demanding the death penalty for those Covenanters captured in the battle.

Sharp showed his true colours as President of the court when he addressed eleven prisoners who had surrendered on a promise of mercy? "You were pardoned as soldiers, but you are not acquitted as subjects." Sharp had the men executed, their hands and right arms were to be struck off, their hands were to be fixed at the city gates and their arms were to be fixed to the prison doors. When Charles II wrote a letter demanding that no more lives be taken from the captives, Sharp held on to the letter, thus ensuring the hundreds more would be put to death.

Sharp also was instrumental in appointing William Carmichael as the Sheriff Depute of Fife. Carmichael was a dissolute man, who spent his time drinking, but he was exceptionally zealous in persecuting the Covenanters so he could impose fines and secure their possessions.

The Earl of Lauderdale saw that affairs in Scotland had become really bad and Sharp's policies must be restrained. Lauderdale took charge and the execution of Covenanters ceased for a time.

On 11 July 1668, Sharp was in Edinburgh with Bishop Honeyman (a former minister of Holy Trinity) when there was an attempted assassination. A Covenanter, James Mitchell bought a pistol and shot at Sharp in his carriage. He hit Honeyman instead. Honeyman lived for a year, but ultimately died from the wounds. Mitchell was later executed.

After the attempted assassination things became quiet for a time. Lauderdale passed the Act of Supremacy, giving the king control of ecclesiastic matters. Then in 1676 a Proclamation against conventicles was issued. There was a seizure of ministers/preachers and the families who did not attend church were fined. There was also a Committee of Public Affairs with wide ranging powers. In 1679, Sharp introduced a very evil piece of legislation. It permitted the killing of any person who was armed, either going to or coming from a conventicle. The killing was to take place without trial.

More stories about Archbishop Sharp

About 1673 Archbishop Sharp was preaching in St Andrews citing passages "whoremongers and adulterers." Isobel Lindsay rose up in church and charged him with guilt. She was removed and gagged for some days. [13] The gag was a very nasty instrument called the branks, which was placed over her head to stop her speaking.

George Barclay was at St Andrews, when Archbishop Sharp gave his first sermon as Archbishop in Holy Trinity. Sharp said "I could have lived with Presbyterians but their divisions were so great that the King saw fit to set up Episcopacy and has been pleased to name me for this see. Those that will not submit shall be forced by the sword and the law.[14]

The inventors of torture instruments

Archbishop Sharp was a nasty piece of work. He introduced the "branks", an evil instrument, which was put on the head of a woman to stop her speaking. Bishop Paterson was just as bad a man and is known as the inventor of thumbscrews.

Sharp did well out of being an Archbishop, as he bought the estate of Scotscraig in Tayport. As well as being cruel, he was mercenary.

Archbishop Sharp and the persecution of two Covenanters

The Duke of Rothes appeared to be severe in his persecution of the Presbyterians in order to please Sharp and the clergy. He invited archbishop Sharp to dine with him. The Archbishop complained about two of the Duke's tenants David and James Walker, who were helpers and supporters of conventicles. He was very angry. The Duke was surprised and said that he would attend to the matter. The Archbishop insisted that he might not forget them, so the Duke immediately gave orders to his servants to go to Leslie and bring them to him after dinner and promised the Archbishop that they should

---

[13]   15 Analecta page 300 1715
[14]   Analecta page 300 1

give the Government no more trouble. The two men were apprehended and brought to one of the rooms in Leslie. The Duke saw the Archbishop to his coach and the Archbishop gave him a reminder about the two men and said that they should be dealt with severely. The Duke had a conversation with the two men and dismissed them. The Duchess was worried about the men and asked a servant to bring them to her. In tears and trembling she asked them what had happened "Nothing but kindness " they said. (Normally the Duke of Rothes was neither kind nor merciful but perhaps he had enough of Sharp's vindictiveness) [15]

Archbishop Sharp's murder

A group of Fife Covenanters decided to assassinate William Carmichael, the sheriff who was engaged in carrying out Sharp's orders and enriching himself in the process. Carmichael was the main target of the assassins, but hid himself when he learned of the plot. But the assassins learned of Sharp who was staying overnight in Kennoway on his way to St Andrews. They assembled at Magus Moor a few miles from the town.

The local Covenanters were David Hackston from Rathillet, John Balfour from Kinloch (near Collessie) James Russell from Kettle, George Fleming Junior from Balbuthie (Kilconquhar) George Balfour from Gilston (Largo parish) Andrew and Alexander Henderson sons of John Henderson of Kilbrackmont (Kilconquhar parish) and Andrew Gullan. Some authorities name Robert Dingwall and William Daniel (addresses unknown). The men heard that Archbishop Sharp would be passing but they knew that his daughter was in the coach with him and were unwilling to do her harm and they demanded that Sharp come out of the coach. But he refused, so they shot at him and thrust at him with their swords. Balfour told Sharp that they were not killing him from personal malice but for causing the death of the Covenanters. They shot him again and one stabbed him. Sharp crawled out of the coach and asked Hackston, who was mounted on a horse and asked for protection. Hackston said that he would not lay a hand on him but the others with swords killed him.

---

[15]   Analecta 4 Page 410

The Covenanters escaped and all except two (Gullan accidentally and Hackston after the Battle of Drumclog) were never caught. The hand of David Hackston, one of Sharp's murderers is buried in St Michael's churchyard in Cupar. David Hackston was executed July 30 1680 at Bothwell Bridge and his hand was cut off. The story of Gullan is given below.

Archbishop Sharp was buried illegally in Holy Trinity church after an enormous funeral paid for by the King. The nasty Bishop Paterson preached his funeral sermon.

An enormous memorial sits in Holy Trinity today. Archbishop Sharp's son erected it in 1680. The inscription reads as follows:

Deo Optimo Maximo, to God, the best and the greatest.

This lofty mausoleum protects

The most precious ashes of a most holy Prelate, a

Most sagacious Senator, a most sacred Martyr;

For here lies

All that remains under the sun of James Sharp

Doctor of Divinity, most Reverend Father in Christ,

Archbishop of St Andrews, Primate of all Scotland, etc

Who was seen, recognised and admired

As a professor of Philosophy and Theology by the University

As a priest, a doctor and a Chief Priest by the Church

As a Prime Minister in Ecclesiastical as in civil affairs by Scotland

As an advocate of the restoration of the monarchical

Rule of the most serene Charles the Second by Britain,

As a renewer of the order of Bishops in Scotland by the Christian world,

As an example of piety, an Angel of Peace, an Oracle

Of wisdom, and an image of Gravity by Good

And faithful subjects and as a most keen enemy of

Impiety, of treachery and Schism by the

Enemies of God, the King and the Flock;

And yet who
For all that he was of such a kind and so great
Was slaughtered in a horrid manner,
Having fallen on his knees that he might yet pray
For his own people;
He was pierced through by very many wounds of
Pistols, swords and daggers,
By nine forsworn parricides excited by fanatical
Rage in the full sunlight of midday in the vicinity
Of his own metropolitan city
In spite of the tears and protests of his most dear
First born daughter,
And of his domestic servants, who had been
Wounded; on the third day of May 1679, 61 years of age.

Alternative translation

.......Enemies of God, the King and the people as the bitterest foe of
irreligion, treason and schism and whom, despite his character and eminence,
nine sworn assassins, inspired by fanatical rage, did with pistols, swords and
daggers most foully massacre close to his metropolitan seat, under the noonday
sun with his beloved eldest daughter and his personal attendants bleeding,
weeping and protesting, on May 3rd 1679 in the sixty-first year of his age,
piercing him with countless wounds when he had fallen on his knees to pray for
his murderers...

A final verdict on Archbishop Sharp

"For well conducted, cold blooded systematic dissimulation he stands
almost without a match in history." (Dodds the fifty year struggle)

There have been attempts to rehabilitate Sharp, but they all fail on one
point the words "forgiveness and compassion". He did not seem to pay attention
to the story of Jesus and the woman taken in adultery. He was ruthless and

merciless when he could have saved many Covenanters lives had he been a more merciful kinder man. Julia Buckroyd said he acted like a politician, but all too often he did not act as a servant of Jesus. That alone condemns him.

A memorial to Archbishop Sharp

There is a pyramid in Magus Woods nine feet high with an inscription, which reads in Latin: "Near this place, James, Archbishop of St Andrews, by safe enemies, with his daughter standing by, was slaughtered. Pray. 1679.

Revenge for Archbishop Sharp's murder

As a revenge for the murder of Archbishop Sharp, five Covenanters captured at Bothwell Bridge were executed, although they had nothing to do with the murder of the Archbishop. A memorial to the five men stands in a field near to the monument for Archbishop Sharp.

The inscription reads as follows:

Here lies Thos Brown,

James Wood, Andrew Sword,

John Weddell, John Clyde,

Who suffered martyrdom on Magus Moor

for their adherence to the word of God and Scotland's covenanted Reformation

November 25 1679

The escape of a Covenanter (George Balfour of Gilston) [16]

Andrew Watson, a farmer occupied Kinaldy, while a nephew of Archbishop Sharp was the nominal laird (he was confined in an asylum). On 3 May 1679, Peggy Watson, the farmer's daughter was out with a neighbouring lad when she saw a man dragged from a coach and murdered. She told her father. At 10 o'clock at night, when the family were at their prayers, a young man came to the door and said, "hide me". Andrew Watson said "George

---

[16]   Anonymous Tales and Sketches of the Covenanters page 142

Balfour, would the woods at Gilston not hide you?" The young man replied that the soldiers were looking for him and he could not go home. Andrew Watson said, "follow me" and he went to the barn and took a sack, half filled it with straw, put the young man inside and put straw on top. The straw was loose so he could breathe. Andrew Watson then placed the sack sideways amongst the others. Andrew Watson told the young man to stay until morning. Meantime a company of dragoons received directions to where George Balfour had fled. The dragoons came to Kinaldy and searched the entire steading and house and even let loose all the livestock. One dragoon came across the sacks of oats and emptied one out for his horses. But they could not find George Balfour. However they terrorised the oldest girl so she admitted that the fleeing George Balfour had been there. The dragoons then threatened to set fire to the steading but were prevented in doing so because a message came that Balfour of Burley (Kinloch) was seen at Dura Den. They hastened there to find that he had escaped. Meantime George Balfour went from Kinaldy to Kenly Den and thence to Elie, where he boarded a ship for the continent.

Poor Andrew Watson was badly treated for his part in the escape. He had all his possessions forfeited and was declared an outlaw and turned out of his house and farm. He sought shelter with his nephew in Auchtermuchty in vain. Finally he was helped by Lord Crawford and given a house and job for himself and his wife at Struthers Castle.

The mystery of the bones

The bones of Archbishop Sharp are not beside his memorial, as they were apparently removed during a break into the church in 1720. The Kirk Session probably knew who removed the bones and the speculation is how far did they engineer it or take a blind eye to the removal. When the church was being renovated in 1829, workmen looked for the bones below the tomb and found none and hence the supposed removal during the break-in. But the mystery is further complicated that there was a further renovation being carried out in the ministry of the Rev Dr Boyd. When Dr Boyd and Principal Shairp looked at the hole below the tomb, Principal Shairp held up a jawbone and said this was the jawbone of Archbishop Sharp. Are some of his bones still in the tomb today? And why leave a jawbone if you wish to dispose of Archbishop Sharp altogether or was it just carelessness or misfortune that a bone was left? A possible alternative explanation is that the bone or bones left were those of Archbishop Gladstanes, who was also buried in the church. A possible motive for the removal of the bones (apart from Archbishop Sharp being a hated figure) is that the Archbishop should not have been buried in the church in the first place, as this was an illegal act. The Kirk Session acted illegally in allowing this burial.

The fate of a Covenanter and his memorial Andrew Gullan

His memorial stone is at Site NO 45845 14549 in a few trees west of Claremont farm.

There is an inscription, which reads as follows:

Memorial stone to Andrew Gullan, who suffered at the gallows in Edinburgh or St Andrews (the accounts differ) and afterwards was "hung upon a pole and lieth here" (i.e. near to Magus Moor). He was executed in 1683 for being present at the scene of the murder of Archbishop Sharp). He had escaped but was discovered working on a Sunday at a farm in the Lothians and arrested.

The inscription reads as follows:
A faithful Martyr here doth lie
A witness against perjury
Who cruelly was put to death
To gratify proud prelates wrath
They cut his hands ere he was dead
And after that struck off his head
To Magus Muir they did him bring
His body on a pole did hing

His blood under the alter cries

Fix vengeance on Christ's enemies

Erected 1738

17th century gifts

Some generous gifts were made to the church at that time as follows:

John Carstairs, Provost of St Andrews and his wife Eupham Shevez gave three communion cups. John Carstairs was Provost between 1622 and 1635.

Another Communion cup of 1659 was given by Barbara Geddie, widow of Patrick Geddie, the minister of Orwell and two more cups were given by a bequest of Baillie James Carstairs in 1671 in the name of himself and his wife Christine Brydie.

A baptismal basin and laver by Archbishop Sharp in 1675 for the use of the parish of the city of St Andrews.

Revolution 1688

The **Revolution** in 1688 and the accession of William III put an end to bishops in the Church of Scotland. The Act of Supremacy was repealed in 1690. The new settlement restored the General Assembly but it was subject to Parliament by statute. The Church of Scotland was now allowed to run its own affairs.

The Revolution settlement had to be read in all churches and two ministers were deposed for not reading the proclamation, because they were Episcopalians.

John Wood MA

John Wood MA was born in 1651 and his father was Provost of St Salvators College. He was ordained on 3 November 1686 and was inducted into the second charge of Holy Trinity on 9 November 1686, being presented by the Town Council. His sentence of deposition was on 11 May 1689 for not reading the proclamation of the Estates. He died in June 1703.

Richard Waddell MA DD

Richard Waddell MA DD was born in 1630 and graduated from St Andrews University in 1648. He was ordained at Dunbar in 8 September 1657 and ministered at Stenton from 6 October 1658 until 1660, at Kelso from 14 May 1660 until 1682 and St Mungo's Glasgow from 28 March 1682 until 1684. He was rector of the University of Glasgow between 1682 and 1684. He came to the First Charge of Holy Trinity St Andrews on 10 July 1684 and was presented by Archbishop Burnet. He was therefore a highly experienced minister when he came to St Andrews and was rector of St Andrews University 1686-1689. He was deposed on 11 May 1689 because he did not read the proclamation of the Estates. He returned under an amnesty in 1703. The church was not happy with him because of his Episcopalian views and an agent (it is not clear who this was) took out letters of horning against him (effectively declaring him an outlaw) and banishing him from St Andrews. He was a DD of St Andrews University. He died on 11 June 1718.

Mr. Haddo at St Andrews said that there were several of the outed clergy at St Andrews. One is Strachan, who had the English Service and his congregation was not very numerous. He joined with Archdeacon Waddell and when upon the toleration, Waddell began and prayed for the Queen and Hanover. They separated again and set up a distinct meeting with the English service. Lately he told me, Forsyth was reading prayers. Haddo said that he did not know whether by trick or oversight Waddell read the petitions for Queen Anne and Sophia. The hearers were not happy and sat down and rose when the prayer was over. Several complained and intended to leave but Waddell said it was a mistake and the book led him to do it.

The three remaining bishops consecrated three clergymen, Waddell, Strachan and a third.[17]

James Rymer or Rymour

---

[17] Analecta page 50 1712

James Rymer or Rymour, (1689-1697) who was a minister at the General meeting of Presbyterians in July 1687, was one of two men who replaced the banned ministers. He came from St Salvator's College where he was appointed as a visitor on 4 July 1690. He was appointed to Holy Trinity in 1690. He died on 26 April 1697.

Thomas Forrester

Thomas Forrester, (1692-1698), who was minister of Killearn replaced the other banned minister. He was inducted into Holy Trinity in 1692 and was translated to St Mary's College in St Andrews in 1698.

John Anderson MA,

John Anderson MA, was minister of the first charge of Holy Trinity. He was born in 1655 and graduated MA (Edinburgh) in 1672. He was ordained as a preacher in the Synod of Lothian and Tweeddale on 6 July 1687. He was inducted to the charge of Earlston on 4 October 1687 and was translated to St Cuthbert's, Edinburgh in 1691. He was called to the First Charge of Holy Trinity on 25 June 1698 and admitted 16 July 1699. He died in February 1712.

Alexander Shields MA

Alexander Shields MA was the next minister. He was born in 1661. He graduated MA of Edinburgh in 1675. He was ordained in 1684 and he was a preacher in a congregation in Edinburgh. On 11 January 1685, he was arrested preaching in a private house in Cotter Lane, London. His text was from Genesis 49:21 "Napthali is a hind let loose" which became the title of his famous treatise. He was imprisoned in Newgate prison, London, thence to the Edinburgh tolbooth and was imprisoned on the Bass Rock for fourteen months before being released. He was rearrested because he would not give guarantees to refrain from preaching and "Live orderly" and was again a prisoner in the tolbooth in Edinburgh. He escaped by wearing female clothing in November 1686. He then fled to Holland and studied at Utrecht. He collaborated with James Renwick on an Introductory Vindication (of his beliefs). He joined the Church of Scotland on 25 October 1690. He was minister of the Second Charge of Holy Trinity from 15 September 1697 until 1700. He was chaplain to the Cameronians. He took part in the ill-fated Darien expedition, sailing on the Rising Sun on 24 September 1699. He was one of Scotland's first foreign missionaries. He died in Jamaica on his way home on 14 January 1700. He had numerous publications, particularly "a hind let loose".

Chapter 6

Eighteenth century

After the piety, passion and controversy of the previous century the Church of Scotland fell into a deep slumber. On a parish level the Kirk Sessions all too vigorously punished sexual sins often recording them in great detail. There was also sabbatarianism with the observance of the Sabbath rigorously observed. There was the beginning of the industrial revolution, although the largely rural parishes remained intact. The patronage controversies reopened due to the Patronage Act of Queen Anne's reign, with the first of many subsequent dissenters occurring due to the appointment of unpopular ministers or the imposition of strict Calvinist theology. Yet among many people there was a great piety as shown in the poem "The Cottars Saturday night." Agriculture was changing too with the introduction of turnips and Rotation farming.

By the Act of Settlement of 1690 the elders were associated with the appointment which was then ratified or rejected by the whole congregation. However with the union of Parliaments in 1707, there came a change. The Patronage Act of 1712 tore up the previous agreement and patrons once again presented ministers. The Patron of the first charge of Holy Trinity was the Crown and the patron of the second charge of Holy Trinity was the St Andrews Town Council. One minister who had problems with patronage was John McCormick, who seemed content to be presented by the Town Council to the second charge, but when called to the first charge in 1724, he did not accept.

The eighteenth century was a bleak time as passion had left the church. The controlling party was the Moderates and they were content to leave things alone. The town of St Andrews had a lso suffered a sharp decline as trade left the ports on the East Coast and the town sank into decay. The population fell so that there were only 2000 people in St Andrews compared with a population of 15,000 two centuries previously.

William Hardie MA

William Hardie MA was the first eighteenth century minister. He was minister of the second charge of Holy Trinity between 1701 and 1712 and as minister of the first charge between 1712 and 1723. He was a native of St Andrews and the son of the Dean of Guild, who was the precentor of Holy Trinity church. He graduated MA (St Andrews) in 1682. He was the minister of Crail, being inducted in September 1690 before being called to the second charge of Holy Trinity on 9 January 1701 and inducted on 1 May 1701 and translated to the first charge on 6 August 1712. He died on 27 October 1723.

The Kirk Session minutes for the time reveal numerous Kirk Session meetings with Mr Hardie and a few elders (usually 7 or 8) and deacons as well. The main business was money paid to the poor of the parish. The items in the 1715 minutes indicate that there was a huge list of charity cases. One item was a payment for coffins. A schoolmistress from Kinross was given 30 shillings and another payment of 30 shillings was to be shared between two people. The children of a man (Thomas Grant) were only given 12 pence. Charity payments averaged 3- 4 pence. St Andrews was not a wealthy city at this time.

In 1715 there was a rebellion with the Jacobites wishing to put James, the Old Pretender on the throne. The standard of James was raised on the Braes of Mar on 6 September 1715 and Perth was captured on 14 September 1715. The army made its way to Edinburgh but there was an indecisive battle of Sheriffmuir on 13 November 1715 and the rebellion then fizzled out. During the rebellion, some people obtained the keys of the church and tower of St Leonards and rang the bells on the day the Pretender was proclaimed. There appeared to be some sympathy for the Jacobites in St Andrews. There was a great fuss about the church keys in 1716, no doubt as a result of what had happened the previous year.

Other matters included contracts, which would be equivalent of banns for marriage. The remaining items were usually about fornication as this was an attempt to make sure that the upkeep of the children did not fall on the Kirk Session. Often the offenders had to appear before the congregation on the next Sunday on the stool of repentance and say they were sorry for what they had done. One man did not appear and the comment was that he was now in prison. Some fornicators were fined and often it was difficult to make the male offender appear.

Other matters at this time included a collection for the churches in Lithuania, a comment that some children did not go to school. And in 1720 pews were to be fixed in the church.

Alexander Anderson

Alexander Anderson was minister between1725 and 1737 in the First Charge of Holy Trinity. He was born in 1676 and graduated MA in 1697. St Andrews Presbytery licensed him on 22 February 1700. He was minister of Kemback 26 September 1697 and then was inducted as minister of Falkland on 13 May 1703. He was called in April 1724 to Holy Trinity. He was elected minister in November 1724 after competing calls were made to him and to a Mr Smith. The papers were long and the discussion took up two days; at length a great majority of the Commission of Assembly preferred Mr Anderson's call. But several persons were disappointed, as they wanted Mr Smith removed to Edinburgh. On 14 April 1725, at the Commission, Mr Anderson's transportation from Falkland to St Andrews was approved unanimously. Mr Anderson was not much against the move, but left it to the judgement of his brethren.

He was Moderator of the General Assembly in 1735.

At Presbytery, Mr Anderson disapproved of the appointment of Archibald Campbell, Minister of Larbert to the chair of Ecclesiastical History, because there was no guarantee that he would give up the post of Minister of Larbert and

Mr Anderson was concerned that ministers did not have plural appointments. Mr Campbell was eventually appointed and did not come to live in St Andrews.

In 1728 a visitor William Douglas commented on Holy Trinity "a very ancient and stately edifice, built in the figure of a cross with fine freestone and at the West End a handsome spire in good repair." In 1732 another visitor approaching the church from the viewpoint of an Anglican clergyman spoke of "a most elegant and stately monument to Archbishop Sharp" but the church was "a very large building but a small part employed."

In the Assembly of 1730, Mr Anderson was on the other side on the nominations on the Community for Commissions and the nomination of preachers for the General Assembly.

Mr Anderson was in discussion on the errors and infidelity debate of the General Assembly. (Analecta 4 Page 257)

In 1724, Frances Haxton brought another woman, whom he called his wife. (He was brought before the Kirk Session, in a case of adultery or bigamy)

In 1724, proclamations of marriages were costing 20 pence and the money was put in the poor fund.

Mr Anderson died on 9 November 1737.

Laurence Watson MA

Laurence Watson MA was minister of the Second charge from 1712 to 1718. He graduated MA in 1704. He was licensed on 24 January 1711 and was presented by the Town Council on 14 August 1712 and admitted to the Second charge of Holy Trinity on 4 September 1712. He died on 25 August 1718.

John McCormick MA

The next minister was John McCormick MA. He was minister between 1718 and 1752. He was born in 1690. He graduated MA from Edinburgh in 1710 and was licensed by the Presbytery of Dalkeith on 15 September 1716. After the departure of Mr Watson, there were several men preaching and this was presumably with the prospect of being appointed to the vacant charge. On 27

November 1718, there were hearings of John McCormick and William Dalgleish and later the hearing of William Dunlop and John McCormick. George II presented John McCormick to the second charge of Holy Trinity in 12 February 1719 and he was inducted on 7 May 1719. He was a very handsome man when he was appointed "he was one of the prettiest fellows in person and in parts the darling of one sex and the envy of the other" but later became paralysed on the left side. He was called to the first charge in 1724, but did not accept, He was the only minister, who, when called from the second charge to the first charge, did not accept the call.

In May 1726, Mr McCormick was accused by the Dean of Guild of having an affair with the Dean's daughter, apparently without foundation. The Dean of Guild was asked to leave the Kirk Session until he acknowledged his slander. The minister was to prosecute the family before the Commission Court. Because of the upset, there was no communion in the church.

Mr. McCormick accepted the call to the first charge for the second time on 26 April 1738. During his ministry in the first charge, the roof was repaired in 1749. He died on 29 December 1752.

John Hill

John Hill was a preacher in Edinburgh, who was called to the Second charge of Holy Trinity on 20 July 1738 and was presented by the Town Council to the second charge of Holy Trinity on 2 November 1738. George II presented him to the first charge of Holy Trinity and he was translated on 27 June 1753. He died after a long illness on 18 November 1764.

David Craigie

David Craigie, who was born in 1722 in St Monans, a graduate of St Andrews University, was licensed on 29 August 1745. He was presented by the Town Council to the Second Charge of Holy Trinity in August 1753 and admitted on 31 January 1754. He died on 4 February 1757.

James Gillespie DD

James Gillespie DD was the next minister of the first charge. He came from Dunbarney, and was presented by the Town Council and ordained to the second charge in 1757. He was then translated from the second charge to the first charge on 12 June 1765 and was appointed Principal of St Mary's on 3 October 1779. He obtained the degree of DD from St Andrews. He was Moderator of the General Assembly in 1779.

Items from Kirk Session minutes:

1758 After Sederunt James Gillespie and John Hill.

Mrs. Symons had been guilty with George Philip, who had since died. She was anxious to have her scandal purged and hoped that the Session would call her before them.

1769 George Lawson, after being seriously exhorted and interrogated, denied he was the father of Alison Kay's child and that any indecent familiarity had ever passed between them. Alison Kay was likewise called. The Session will consider this affair at a further opportunity. (the result was not known)

Mrs. Amy Dempster asked the Session to grant her the seat previously occupied by Mrs. O'Mary upon her leaving this place. The matter lay on the table.

Thomas Aikman, farmer was the father of Ann Fyals child. He would have been guilty with her about the end of December. And a second time he fornicated in his father's barra in the West Wynd, when she was going about her master's business.

Marjery Small, a widow and unmarried, having been cited to this diet and acknowledged hat she was with child and being suitably exhorted and interrogated, she declared that William Aitken, married, was the father of her child. He had been guilty with her in her own house about the end of July. Lastly he had frequented her house much in the twelve months past. William Aitken, having also been cited, was called and compered. She was cited to attend the Session tomorrow at 10 o'clock. The beddal was ordered to cite the said William

Aitken, the same day. William Aitken was likewise called, having been seriously exhorted to be truthful and interrogated, he owned he was the father of her child. The Session appointed them to begin their public appearance next Sunday, the widow in the forenoon and the man in the afternoon. Marjorie Small, having been cited in this was called and compered. She adhered to her former declaration that William Aitken was the father of her child.

Thomas Aikman being variously exhorted had continued to deny his guilt and it was alleged that he was known to associate with people of bad character. They were brought together before the Session and confessed that she will continue to accept him, referring the charge of keeping bad company and continue to deny his guilt. The woman acknowledged that she had never notified him that she was with child within a day or two of her being delivered

1770 Richard Paton and his wife Ann Paton left this parish in Martinmas, having been resided in the same parish several years free from public scandal or church censure, so that nothing is known to hinder their reception in any Christian congregation where Providence may take their lot. Robert Bogie (Minister) and Sam Morrison (Session Clerk) attest this. Did they go to St Andrews or why was it in the St Andrews minutes?

1774? Gentlemen I (Thomas Roger) received on Thursday last a summons from the Moderator requiring me to answer to a charge against me by Anne Hutton of having been guilty of sex with her. She had declared (not clear what she said)....

Thomas Roger was accused of fornication with Anne Hutton. He made a representation to the Session. He was sent to the place by his father to prosecute his studies in philosophy. His father wished him to maintain an irreproachable character and he humbled himself at the thoughts of his father's displeasure if he heard of this accusation. The session were too well acquainted with the character of my accuser to think that she derived much credit but also at the distance at which he lived from his accuser.

She had declared that she heard Anne Hutton say to Mr. Rogers in his house if she should give her a line for money, she would find another father for her child. If not she would name him the father. (She said) that the Declarant's wife asked him to go to the door with her and leave Mr. Rogers and Anne Hutton together, lest they should have something to say together in private, but that Mr. Roger insisted on his wife staying as he cared not that the whole world heard. So what was to be between him and Anne Hutton that he had often seen Mr. Rogers but never saw him in so great a passion before, to which Anne Hutton replied that the cause of his passion was that so many people were going about her.

Agnes Roger was called in and being interrogated if ever she saw Anne Hutton and Mr. Rogers being together and answered they never did but once in her own house. She replied her own husband Thomas Coupar did only more circumstantially.

Christian Simson was called in and being interrogated said that she saw Mr. Rogers and Anne Hutton together in Thomas Coupar's house and declared on all parts as Thomas Coupar had done.

The Session, having taken the whole affair into consideration and in respect of Anne Hutton deliberated the matter. (The result was to be given in a future meeting.)

The matter seems too trivial to come before the Kirk Session.

David Hunter MA DD

David Hunter MA DD was born in 1724 and graduated MA in 1745. He came from Monimail and was licensed in 1750. He was minister of Monimail in 1752 and was presented by the Town Council to the Second Charge of Holy Trinity on 17 October 1765. He was a DD of St Andrews in 1769 and died on 4 November 1771. He had a number of publications including "Observations on the history of Jesus Christ serving to illustrate the propriety of his conduct over the beauty of his character."

John Adamson MA DD

John Adamson MA DD was born in 1742 at Leuchars and graduated MA at St Andrews in 1757. St Andrews Presbytery licensed him on 7 March 1763. On 7 May 1764, he was admitted to the charge of Kilmany. He obtained the degree of DD (St Andrews) in 1777. He was presented by the Town Council and was admitted to the Second Charge of Holy Trinity in 1773 and then presented to the first Charge of Holy Trinity on 21 October 1779 and translated to the first charge on 15 December 1779. He became the Moderator of the General Assembly in 1797. He died of apoplexy (a stroke) after preaching the sermon in the church in 1808.

His sole publication was "A sermon preached on then anniversary of the Revolution."

He was the writer of the First Statistical account of St Andrews parish. The stipend was 14 bolls of wheat, 3 firlots, 2 pecks, 2.5 lippies, of barley and also 63 bolls 3 firlots. A calculation makes his stipend about 13 tonnes of cereals. The stipend of the second charge was 1300 merks. As a merk was equal to 13.5 pence sterling, the total stipend of the second charge amounted to £45.50, which could be compared with a farm workers wage of £7 per year. There was no manse. There were 47 poor, who received money from the collections. The congregation amounted to 2390 persons and there were 91 dissenters. The usual number of communicants was 1500-1600. There were 40 persons over 80 years of age and one in Boarhills was over 90.

Item from Kirk Session minutes:

1785 Isobel Ramsay made an appearance before the congregation for the sin of fornication and accordingly was rebuked twice and dismissed from censure.

Buildings

The church was re-roofed in 1749 and a number of repairs were done in 1767. However, the church was insufficient for the members so it was completely remodelled in 1798-1800 and large galleries were added so that the church could now seat 3000 people. The architect was Robert Balfour. The new layout lasted until 1907-1909 and pictures of the church in this period are on display in the church. The layout was not satisfactory, as 500 of the congregation could not see the minister. These pews were called "Believers pews" because of this. (Dr Boyd, at a later date queried this statement) The absence of the East window made the church very dark. The old gallery which was called "the sailors loft" and which was dated 1580 was sold to the burgher church in 1798.

Chapter 7

19th century

Introduction

The century began with the Church of Scotland and two dissenting Presbyterian churches, the Original Secession Church and the Relief Church, both of which began in the previous century as a result of the patronage question. (The rights of patrons, usually landowners, to appoint the ministers without regard to what the parishioners thought about the new minister). The patronage question lingered on until 1874, when the Government allowed a bill to abolish the system but only because of the great disruption of 1843, which set up the Free Church. The Relief church and most of the Original Succession church amalgamated to become the United Presbyterian Church. Thus in 1899 St Andrews had four Presbyterian Churches, two Church of Scotland, one Free Church (Martyrs) and one United Presbyterian (Hope Park). Worship had changed in the nineteenth century. The times of the services changed from 11 a.m. and 2 p.m. to 11 a.m. and 6 p.m. Also instrumental music, either an organ or harmonium, was installed instead of having a precentor with a tuning fork. Hymns were sung, instead of the praise entirely consisting of psalms and paraphrases. A new hymnbook was authorised, lessons were read from the Bible and the sermon length decreased but was still about ½ hour at the end of the century. No longer were the parents of illegitimate children hauled up before the Kirk Session. The population and church membership had increased but was now split between three fairly equal denominations, leaving a loss in authority of the Parish Churches. The Fast Days were abandoned and replaced with evening preparatory services. Christmas and Easter were celebrated for the first time since the Reformation but were still not a holiday.

Theology and Biblical Studies were in ferment due to the new Biblical Criticism in Biblical Studies and scientific discoveries, particularly the theory of Evolution. The old Westminster Catechism came under attack mainly because of the doctrine of election and everlasting punishment, which was felt to be unchristian. There was also controversy over the literal interpretation of some books of the Bible, particularly, the first five books of the Old Testament. There were several prominent cases of heresy, the last in 1897. These cases involved ordained ministers, either parish ministers or professors. However these cases are unlikely to have affected the main bulk of church members, unlike the problems of greatly disliked ministers intruded on congregations.

The Free Church of Scotland and the United Presbyterian Church were united in 1900.

Bells of the church

One of the bells of the church was not in use so it was taken to St Paul's cathedral in about 1800. The Town Council ordered a new bell in 1807 but it was not properly hung and so lay unused till at 8 a.m. on 1 January 1846, when the inhabitants of St Andrews were surprised to be wakened by the bells.

George Hill DD

George Hill DD, the son of John Hill, was born in St. Andrews in 1750. Hill graduated from the University of St. Andrews in 1764, and in 1787, St. Andrews awarded him the Doctor of Divinity degree. He was appointed to the second charge in 1780. However his appointment was unsuccessfully opposed, as it was felt that dual appointments of university professors and church ministers to a single post was not proper. This was partly due to a change in attitudes from the moderate view to an evangelical outlook. At the age of twenty-two, St. Andrews appointed him to a professorship in Greek, which he held for sixteen years alongside his ministerial duties (1772-1788). In 1788, St. Andrews appointed him Professor of Divinity in St. Mary's College, and in 1791, the University promoted him to the position of Principal of St. Mary's College.

Hill was an eloquent speaker and successful literary figure, and he published several books and essays. In addition to his Sermons (1796), his publications included Lectures upon Portions of the Old Testament (1812),

Theological Institutes (1817), and Lectures on Divinity, 3 volumes. (1821). In his 1790 "Sermon XIV," Hill challenged the General Assembly of the Church of Scotland to the universal spread of the Christian message. Only two years, later, William Carey published his famous essay An Enquiry into the Obligations of Christians to Use Means for the Conversion of the Heathens, which argues for the same outcome as Hill's sermon. Professor Hill was Dean of the Order of the Thistle from 1787, Dean of the Chapel Royal from 1799 and Moderator of the General Assembly 1788. When Mr Adamson died in 1808, George Hill was appointed Minister of the first charge. The Prince Regent presented him to the charge in 1808. He was Rector of Edinburgh University.

As well as being Moderator of the General Assembly for one year, he was for many years, leader of the Moderate party. This party could be summed up as being the party of enlightened Calvinists and Presbyterians, who were prepared to compromise with the Government on many matters, but not on the spiritual independence of the church. Hill said "The Church of Scotland is independent of any party and any ministry: he cared not for the threats of the learned gentleman (the Lord Advocate) and he might tell his friends so." He opposed a levy during the Napoleonic wars as being too political.

In 1805 Admiral Nelson died at Trafalgar and there was a detailed account in the Kirk Session minutes.

In 1807, returning from the General Assembly, he took ill, probably had a fit. In 1816, he began to decline with attacks of apoplexy, but continued to preach, leaving his assistant with his parochial work. In 1819, he stumbled when leaving the pulpit and thereafter never preached again.

George Hill died in December 19 1819 aged 69.

Dr Hill "was a kindly, humorous but serious man, who was loved by his family and his congregation" according to his biographer George Cook.

Robert Haldane DD

Robert Haldane DD was Dr Hill's successor in the First Charge of Holy Trinity. He was born in 1772 in Overtown near Lecropt and studied at Glasgow and St Andrews Universities. He was minister of Drumelzier and was ordained on 9 March 1807. He resigned in 1809 when he was appointed Regius Professor of Mathematics in St Andrews University. He was an excellent teacher of mathematics. He was unsuccessful at obtaining the Chair of Mathematics at Edinburgh University. He became Professor of Theology in the University of St Andrews on 21 September1820 and also became minister of the first charge of Holy Trinity in 1820, being presented by the Prince Regent. Sir David Brewster, Principal of United College had a vendetta against him. However Dr Haldane put up a sturdy defence of the physical and financial administration of the College. He was elected a fellow of the Royal Society of Edinburgh in 1820. He was Moderator of the General Assembly in 1827. He published a pamphlet on poverty in St Andrews in 1841.

Haldane was unmarried. He was extremely kind to young women. He never became annoyed with them. When a pretty girl said to him" Principal why do you say everything three times. Principal Haldane replied looking at her *Well Miss Jeanie, I do repeat, I do repeat, I do repeat." Miss Jeanie was silent.

Dr Boyd said that Haldane was a wonderfully amiable man .A parishioner said that he was not amiable at all. He said that Haldane was worse tempered than Dr Boyd and Dr Park put together. Principal Haldane could be somewhat peppery.

His character was summed up "He was of unceasing charity. His heart was entirely on the well being of his students. "(Conolly)

Principal Haldane died on 9 March 1854 and lies buried in the Cathedral Cemetery.

Mr Cook (the church advocate) was advocate in a case where the phrase "dry sermons" was used. He went on at length about the meanings of dry such as a "dry day" but he said that you could not have a dry sermon. The opposing advocate said to Mr Cook that he had been brought up in St Andrews and did not know the meaning of a dry sermon (Dr Haldane's and Dr Hill's sermons were notorious for being too academic.)

George Buist DD

George Buist DD was minister of the Second Charge of Holy Trinity. He was minister of Falkland between 1802 and 1813. He was called to Holy Trinity in 1809, but only admitted to Holy Trinity in 1813 after litigation. The litigation was over the teinds of St Andrews and it was settled that none of the teinds was to be allocated to the ministry of the Second Charge. The Town Council presented him to the charge. He was minister until 1860. He became professor of Hebrew in 1817, holding the post along with being minister of the Second Charge. He was Moderator of the General Assembly in 1848. He died in April 1860.

St Mary's

The church was still insufficient for the members due to the expanding burgh and an overflow church (St Mary's) was established in 1839-1840 and the services there were taken by the two ministers in turn. The church seated 560 people. It is now the Victory Memorial Hall.

Statistical account

The new statistical account was written in 1841. There were 2490 persons on the common roll and 697 dissenters. There were 328 persons of the United Associate Synod, 150 Burghers, 108 Episcopalians and 111 independents and one Roman Catholic family. The average number of communicants was 2030. The total population of the parish was 6017 in 1831 and 6571 in 1841. The church collections for the poor amounted to £417. Poor people received from 6d to 2/6 per week. There were 1626 baptisms, 1778 marriages and 1740 deaths (These figures seem rather dubious unless they are for several years). There was no manse or glebe and the stipend was 28.5 chalders of grain (about 75 tonnes of grain). The minister of the second charge received £75–4-5 ½ plus 107 bolls of grain (about 18 tonnes) +teinds on fish, but this was not paid due to the poverty of the fishermen with an addition of £31–10–5 and an allowance in lieu of manse and glebe. There was also a catechist.

Disruption

The disruption of 1843 happened when a large number of ministers and a third of members of the Church of Scotland walked out and formed the Free Church. In St Andrews this church was Martyrs Church. The numbers were small in St Andrews, as there were only 30 members, who met to set up the church, unlike many other places where many or sometimes nearly all the members left to form the Free Church.

In St Andrews the ministers of Holy Trinity, Dr Haldane and George Buist did not join the Free Church, but stayed with the Church of Scotland. They did so, believing that a revitalised national church was the best solution to church problems.

John Park DD

John Park DD was Dr Haldane's successor to the first charge between 1854 and 1865. He was born in Greenock on 14 January 1804. He was licensed in 1831 and was at the West church Greenock, Bonhill, Rodney Street Presbyterian Church Liverpool and in 1843, Glencairn church. Queen Victoria presented him to Holy Trinity in 1854. He was of a gentle and retiring disposition. He never married and his life was tinged with some hidden sadness, which no one could make him reveal. There is sadness in many of his songs. Maybe his love died young. It is said that he was a preacher of rare eloquence and an accomplished musician and painter.

He was a composer of songs including the following:

"O gin I were where Gadie rins,"

"The miller's daughter,"

"Montgomery's mistress,"

"Sunshine and swallows,"

"The village bells,"

"The sea song,"

"Yes, thou may'st sigh."

In 1876, after his death, his works were published under the title of "Songs composed and in part written by the late Rev John Park" Leeds 1876. This volume contains a portrait and an introduction by Principal Shairp. It has twenty-seven songs of which both words and music are by John Park and thirty-seven settings by him of words from the great poets. A diary of his visit to Wordsworth at Rydal Mount was published in 1887. His work "Lectures and Sermons" was published in Edinburgh in 1865.

He received the income from some land for the benefit of the poor of the church and this income was used for many years to pay for the rent of needy families and was distributed by the St Andrews ministers.

Dr Park lived in his own house at 4 Hope Street.

He was President of the St Andrews Choral society. One night, at the choral society, when the Hallelujah chorus began Dr Park stood up and said "Is this not glorious?" and then collapsed and said to his doctor "Is this not death?" He died the next morning, 8 April 1865.

Alexander Hill

Alexander Hill became minister of the Second Charge of Holy Trinity after the death of George Buist. He was born on 28 January 1826 and was educated at Glasgow University. He was ordained on 20 December 1849 and was previously minister of Kilsyth. He was minister of the second charge of Holy Trinity from 11 October 1860 until his death on 5 January 1875. The Kirk Session minutes said he was "kindly and had a genial manner." He also "was sound and faithful in preaching and diligent in pastoral duty and care of the sick, the young and the elderly and had the regard and the esteem of the community." His sudden death was a great loss to the church.

Andrew Kennedy Hutchison Boyd BA DD LLD

Andrew Kennedy Hutchison Boyd BA DD LLD was Dr Park's successor in the first charge of Holy Trinity. He was born in Auchinleck in November 1825 and was originally destined for a law career, but became a minister. He was minister of St George's Edinburgh, Newton on Ayr, Kilpatrick Irongray and St Bernard's Edinburgh and was inducted minister of the first charge on 14 September 1865. There were 1000 people at his induction.

In his first year Dr Boyd visited everyone in the parish amounting to 8000 people.

Dr Boyd took ill in January 1871, and when he recovered, he was obliged to rest for the next three Sundays and he was ordered to work less for six months. When he preached again, he had the lessons read for him for six months.

He was Moderator of St Andrews Presbytery in 1870 for 6 months. He was Moderator of the General Assembly in 1890. The ladies of the congregation presented Dr Boyd with his Moderator's robes on May 18 1890. Dr Boyd lived in his own house at 7 Abbotsford Crescent.

Author

He was a well known author and wrote books:

The autumn holidays of a Country Parson. 1865

The Critical Essays of a Country Parson.1865

Recreations of a country parson. 1889

Leisure Hours in town. 1882

The Commonplace philosopher in town and country. 1865

Lessons of middle age with some account of various cities and men.

Landscapes churches and moralities.

Our little life: Essays consolatory and domestic. 1889

St Andrews and elsewhere. (Reprint) 2009.

The Church of the Waldensis.

Our homely comedy and tragedy. 1887

East Coast days and memories.

Graver thoughts of a country parson.

Twenty five years in St Andrews 1865-1890 (2 volumes) 1892

The last years of St Andrews. 1896

Occasional and Immemorial days. 1895

To meet the day through the Christian year

The best last: with other chapters to help. 1885

What set him right: with other chapters to help. 1885

Towards the sunset: teachings after 30 years. 1883

Seaside musings of Sundays and weekdays.

Counsel and Comfort spoken from a city pulpit. 1863

Sunday afternoons at the Parish Church of a Scottish University city.

Changed aspects of unchanged truths.

Present day thoughts and memorials of St Andrews Sundays. 1870

From a quiet place. 1879

A Scotch Communion Sunday. 1873 (In New College Library)

Communion Service (Nineteenth century)

Dr Boyd gave details of a Communion service, probably the one of November 1872. The service must have been very long, possibly about 1.5-2 hours' duration. It included five addresses and the members left the pews in relays to sit at Communion tables. It is not easy today to see where the actual tables were.

A summary of the communion service is given below.

(Sing) Psalm 43 O send thy light forth and Thy truth

Prayer

Reading Isaiah 53 Who hath believed Thy report

(Sing) Psalm 116 I love the Lord

Reading Revelation 5

(Song) Paraphrase 65 Hark how the adoring Host above

Prayer and the Lord's Prayer

Action Sermon Christ crucified

(Sing) Paraphrase 54 I'm not ashamed

Prayer

Apostles Creed

The Fencing of the tables

Reading 1 Corinthians 11 23-29

Welcome to Communion

The Ten Commandments

The Beatitudes

(Sing) Paraphrase 35 'Twas on that night

Elements are carried in

Presiding minister in centre, assisting ministers to the right and left, elders around and the Presiding minister proceeds with the first table service.

Small sermon –women of Sychar

Prayer of Consecration

On that ever memorable night in which our Saviour was betrayed into the hands of sinners, He took bread and having blessed it, as now been done in His name and after His example, He broke bread and gave it to the disciples saying take eat, this is My body which is broken for you: this do in remembrance of Me. In this manner when He had supped He took the cup and gave it to the disciples saying This cup is the New Testament in My blood shed for many for the remission of sins. Drink ye all of it. For as often as ye eat this bread and drink this cup ye do show the Lord's death until He come.

The presiding minister gives first the bread and then the cup to the assisting minister and then the elders. Then the elders carry the consecrated elements to the communicants seated at the tables covered with white cloth.

Entire silence is preserved until all have received.

The minister says a closing statement

(Sing) Psalm 103 2 verses O thou my soul

Communicants depart from Communion tables; the places are filled by others

Table Service 2

Talk

"On that ever memorable night...."

We have taken the cup of Salvation

Go in peace

(Sing) Psalm 103 verses 3 and 4

Table Service 3

Talk and a similar service

(Sing) Psalm 103 verses 5 and 6

Table Service 4

Talk and a similar service

(Sing) Psalm 115 12-18 The Lord make us

Concluding address

Prayer

(Sing) Paraphrase 38 Now Lord according to Thy work

Parting Benediction

Evening Thanksgiving

(Sing) Hymn 1 Holy Holy Holy

Prayer Reading Isaiah 60

(Sing) Hymn 200 We praise Thee O God

Reading John 17 These words

(Sing) Hymn 166 Jerusalem the golden

Sermon John 17: 15

The Saviour's prayer to the first communicants

(Sing) Hymn 148 Abide with me

Prayer

(Sing) Hymn 173 All praise to Thee

Benediction

Communion Services

The twice-yearly Communion services, which were then held in June and December, were a big event in Victorian times. The preparation for Communion involved three Fast Day services on the Thursday preceding the Communion. On Fast days, there were morning and afternoon services in Holy Trinity (Town Church) and morning service only in St Marys from 1874. On Communion Sunday there were morning and afternoon services in both churches with evening thanksgiving in both churches, a total of nine services in all over two days with several visiting ministers. Surprisingly, however the attendances (excluding Boarhills) are similar to the attendance in 1960. Boarhills had separate communion services.

In 1874, it was decided to have only one Communion service in St Mary's in the morning, but to have quarterly Communion services to accommodate those who could not go in the morning service in June and December. It was also decided to have Communion cloths in St Mary's.

The afternoon Fast Day service at Holy Trinity was discontinued with only a morning Fast Day service in both churches in June 1885. In 1887, it was proposed to discontinue the Fast Day services altogether. This happened in 1888 and a service in Holy Trinity only on the Friday evening before Communion was initiated in place of the Fast Day service. This arrangement lasted for over one hundred years.

The dates of the communion services were changed to the First Sunday in May and the first Sunday in November and this is still the arrangement in 2012.

There was only one Communion service in Holy Trinity and one in St Marys for a few years after 1900, but there was also an evening thanksgiving in both churches.

Communion tokens were discontinued in favour of issuing Communion Cards. The first Communion that this was implemented was in June 1887. The elders were made responsible for delivering cards in 1898. (They did not appear very keen to do this)

The practice of sitting at tables in relays was being phased out and when the church was reopened after renovations in 1909, there was no provision for Communion tables. The tables in Victorian times were in the Sharp aisle.

Communion Services in Boarhills

Because there were a number of elderly people in Boarhills who were unable to attend Communion services in Boarhills church, Communion was held in a cottage in Boarhills on Monday 13 December 1881 with Dr Boyd and Dr Anderson. Twelve elderly people attended. This was continued for a number of years.

The ministers had the assistance of one or two visiting ministers to assist with the communion services. One of these was the Rev Professor Flint, Professor of Moral Philosophy and Political Economy at St Andrews University (1864-1873) and Professor of Divinity at Edinburgh University (1873-1903). He preached on September 17 1876. In all, he assisted the Rev A K H Boyd at least sixty times.

Preachers also assisted with the Thursday Fast Day services. Examples include the service on 18 June 1868 when Dr McGregor and Principal Tulloch preached. Also on December 2 1869,when Dr Watson and Dr McGregor (St Cuthberts) preached. Another example was on 16 June 1870, when Dr Watson (Dundee) preached and on Thursday June 15 1871, a Fast Day, Dr Watson, (Dundee) and Dr Young (Monifieth) preached. On Thursday June 13 1877, Dr Lees, (Edinburgh) preached. On Thursday June 17 1880, Mr. Strong (Glasgow Hillhead) and on Thursday December 2 1880, Dr Watson, (Dundee) preached. In 1888, Rev William Proudfoot (St Margaret's, Arbroath) and Rev Mitford Mitchell preached.

On the Communion Sunday itself, in June 1879 Dr McMurtie (St Bernards, Edinburgh) and William Tulloch (Glasgow) preached. On May 1 1892, Dr McMurtie (St Bernards) conducted his 25th Communion Service and

Dr Burns (Glasgow Cathedral) preached at Communion on 26 successive years.

Some other preachers were Rev James Anderson (Kinneff), Rev Spence (Arbroath), Principal Cunningham, Rev James Ewan (Dunino), Rev Finlayson (Burntisland), Rev M Thomson (Memus), Rev John Ferguson (Fern), Rev Baxter (Cameron), Rev Principal Stewart, Rev Wotherspoon, Rev Allan (Monzie), Rev James Craig (Dalgety), Rev Professor Menzies, Rev John Brown (Bervie), Rev Professor Mitchell, Rev Theodore Marshall, and Rev Professor Lawson.

Service times

In 1883, there was a proposal to change the time of the afternoon service from 1.45 p.m. to 2 p.m. The change took place in 1888, as it was a more convenient time and would allow members to go home after the 11 a.m. service. Evening services were to be held at 6.30 p.m. (later at 6 p.m.) The changes from afternoon services to evening services appear to have taken place in the late 1890's.

Buildings

The church was not very convenient and Dr Boyd raised the question of the restoration of the church at a meeting of the heritors on April 19 1869. Dr Boyd was made to feel that the time was not yet ripe. Dr Boyd said that the proposed church restoration should be arranged with ecclesiological propriety and the Communion table should be at the eastern end of the church and the pulpit should be placed at the crossing. This proposal was not fulfilled until the next ministry in 1909.

Some of the seats were known as "Believers pews" as they were inconvenient and the congregation could not see or hear the minister very well. Dr Boyd said that this was nonsense, as everyone could hear him, but perhaps some of the other preachers were not as clearly spoken.

However St Mary's was restored and reopened on October 9 1870. Lessons were read from a lectern, there was a new Communion table, the Te

Deum and Benedictus were sung in the morning and the Magnificat and Nunc Dimittis in the evening.

On May 22 1866, the weathercock was taken down. It was two hundred years old and a new weathercock replaced it.

The church was lit with gas. The lighting was poor. Attempts were made to improve the lighting and larger gas pipes were installed.

Mr Balfour, builder died aged 97 in 1867. He was employed when the church was being remodelled in 1798.

In 1873, improvements to the heating were necessary. Two stoves were replaced at a cost of £373.

A gift of a Communion table was made in 1884.

In 1889, a new window was given by the family of Dr Watson Wemyss of Denbrae in memory of their father and was dedicated on Sunday August 19 1889.

In 1898 a hall was needed for the Boys Brigade. This was eventually erected.

In 1895, a curious complaint was made concerning a pew, which was nailed up at Communion time so the occupant had problems receiving Communion. There was a discussion concerning who gave the order to the Beadle for this to be done. It is not clear whether the matter was resolved to the satisfaction of the pew holder.

New Churches

New churches were settled in Strathkinness in 1864 and Boarhills in 1903, (a preaching station until then), which reduced the pressure on Holy Trinity.

Dean Stanley and other visiting preachers

During his ministry the church entertained various preachers and one who came was the well-known Anglican preacher Dean Stanley, Dean of Westminster. An enormous crowd attended the morning service on 25 August

1872, estimated at 3000. Dean Stanley was not very well as he had a sore throat and received some medication. He did preach the sermon in Holy Trinity, which lasted 1.5 hours. During the procession an old woman with a black umbrella joined in the procession, but the Dean was delighted and not annoyed. A crowd of 500 came to the evening service in St Mary's, but was disappointed that Dean Stanley could only give the benediction.

Not all St Andrews' citizens were pleased. A parishioner to vent his disapproval approached Dr Boyd in the street. He said, "What gart ye bring a Dean to preach in the Toon Kirk on the Sabbath." Dr Boyd answered that the Dean was a great preacher and a great friend of the Church of Scotland. Nevertheless, the man replied "I dinna approve ava' o' ye bringin' a Dean to preach in the Toon Kirk".

Despite this reaction, Dean Stanley preached again in Holy Trinity on Sunday March 16 1877.

Some other visiting preachers were as follows:

January 14 1866, Norman McLeod (Barony) preached. He was one of the most famous ministers of his time.

Sunday 27 February 1870, Professor John Caird preached for 1 hour. He was a very well known preacher, if somewhat obscure.

September 22 1872, Rev Henry De Bunsen (Vicar of Lilleshall) preached. He was a controversial figure, associated with some very strange people.

January 1873, Mr Gillan (Inchinnan) preached.

June 11 1874, Dr Lees (Paisley) preached.

September 27 1874, Signor Cavazzi of Rome preached.

May 1875, Dr Lindsay Alexander, (Augustine Bristo), Edinburgh preached.

March 7 1879, Dr Donald McLeod (Park church, Glasgow) preached on behalf of the Missionary Society.

September 26 1881, Mr Alexander (St Paul's, Walworth) preached in St Mary's.

Thursday August 1 1882 at 1 p.m. Mr Moody preached. This was associated with the second visit of the American revivalists, Moody and Sankey. Although it was a working day 1000 people attended.

March 16 1884, Bishop Wordsworth preached 2000 attended. Bishop Wordsworth was the Bishop of St Andrews and Dunkeld and a well-known hymn writer (two of his hymns are in the present Church of Scotland hymnary). It was the first time in two hundred years, when the local bishop preached in a Church of Scotland church and this was not surprising given the past history of St Andrews Bishops. It does not happen often even now. A harmonium was brought into the church, despite opposition to this instrument from a few of the congregation. The Free Church minister sang in the choir.

Sunday 21 February 1886, Professor Mitchell (Professor of Church History, St Andrews) preached at an evening service and became really worked up about the subject of his sermon. (Scottish church disestablishment)

October 2 1887, Dr Story (Roseneath) preached twice. He was another very prominent Victorian minister.

October 11 1886, Principal Tulloch's last service in St Mary's.

August 25 1889, Dr Grant from Aylesford preached.

Special Services

One of the changes in the Church of Scotland in the late nineteenth century, was the renewal of special services on holy days, which had been abandoned at the Reformation.

The first of these services was a Christmas Service, which was held on a weekday on Christmas 1872 for the first time. Christmas was not a holiday at that time and not until the late 1960's did it become a general holiday. Christmas that year was on a Wednesday. The church was only decorated at Christmas for the first time in 1894. The text of the sermon on that day was "Now let us go even unto Bethlehem."

Other weekday services were beginning to be held on Good Friday and also on Ash Wednesday February 27 1879 (congregation 60). On the

Wednesday service in Holy Week in Easter 1893, between 50 and 60 attended and on the Good Friday of that week, 108 attended. The congregation in 1879 was entirely middle class housewives as it was a normal working day. The pattern of Christmas and Good Friday services continued up to the present time, although these services were often held in the evening.

Praise

The church services included praise, which was either metrical psalms or paraphrases. A precentor led the singing with a tuning fork. He trained his own choir. The members sang sitting down and stood for prayers. A hymnary was introduced into the Church of Scotland in May 1870, called the Scottish Hymnal. This was first used in St Mary's on Sunday August 14 1870. The hymns sung were "Return and come to God" (now found in hymnary.org) and "Holy Holy Holy" (still in the present hymnary). At the evening service the hymn "When our heads are bowed with woe" was sung (now found in the Cyberhymnal). The first time a harmonium was used to sing the praise was in St Mary's on 22 March 1874. The change of the pattern of worship, with the congregation standing for praise and sitting for prayers, came in St Mary's first at the evening service on August 1 1869 and started regularly on May 10 1874. St Mary's was used as a guinea pig for changes that the minister wished to see in Holy Trinity.

Due to the success of the instrumental music in St Mary's, the question of Instrumental music in Holy Trinity was first raised at a Kirk Session meeting on 7 March 1881. The use of a good harmonium was considered, but it was first agreed to consult the view of the congregation. They also agreed that anyone who dissented with the view that a harmonium should be purchased should sign a paper to that effect. Accordingly, a meeting of the congregation was held on 27 March 1882. Only one person, Mr David Henderson, 3 South Street disagreed with the introduction of instrumental music.

At the next meeting of the Kirk Session on 13 April 1882, some procedural difficulties with the congregation meeting were considered. Five members of the Kirk Session proposed that the introduction of the harmonium be delayed. It is not clear whether these people were against the introduction of the harmonium or whether they were just being difficult. However the Kirk Session agreed to continue the matter, with one member Mr John Paterson of Kinburn House dissenting from the resolution of the Kirk Session. On 3 October 1882, the Kirk Session agreed to have a second meeting of the Congregation. The result was the same, with one member against the harmonium.

The Kirk Session then agreed to rent a harmonium. A harmonium was rented. It was not satisfactory. A minute in November 1883, said that a more efficient harmonium was required. A harmonium was purchased for £50 in 1886.

In 1900 Mr Stuart Grace presented a two manual Alexandre harmonium. It is still in the church.

It is not known how the five elders and one member reacted to the purchase of the harmonium. Members then sat (Dr Boyd said kneeled) for prayers. In St Leonards, Principal Shairp stood during the prayers, as he was very conservative and did not support he change in worship.

A new Scottish Hymnal was introduced in the summer of 1885. The Church of Scotland hymnary was introduced in 1898 and is now in the fourth edition.

Pause for prayer.

On July 25 1869, in St Mary's, Dr Boyd suggested that the members pause for silent prayer on entering and leaving the church. There was unseemly haste in leaving the church.

Prayers read

On June 16 1870, an elder said that some of the people said that they did not like the prayers being read. Dr Boyd replied "How did you know that the prayers were read? You could only know by watching the minister rather than praying yourself".

Problems with beadles

Beadle dismissed 1874

The beadle, Mr McKenzie Turpie was sacked for not opening the church on occasions, including the evening service on communion Sunday.

Beadle rebuked

The beadle, Mr. Peattie, had a number of complaints against him for rudeness and one letter in particular from a visitor from Edinburgh, who was very upset at the sheer rudeness of the beadle. The beadle was reprimanded by the kirk Session and told be civil and courteous towards visitors.

Women's Guild

A Women's Guild was established in the Church of Scotland in 1887, resulting in a Guild being founded in Holy Trinity church but not until 25 January 1929. The numbers in the Guild reached 400 in 1940.

Poor persons in parish

In the days before old age pensions and social security there were many people who had no income at all and were in extreme poverty. The church had bequests and made weekly allowances to many people. In addition, in the winter, coal allowances were made to people. Twice yearly in May (e.g. May 13 1879, May 12 1881) and November (e.g. November 11 1879) the two ministers made the rounds of the congregation with a bag of half crowns which were used to pay the rent of poor people in the congregation. The sums given were usually five shillings or seven shillings and six pence. The money came from rents of land, which a previous generous donor had donated to the church in Dr Park's time. There were seventy-seven persons on the poor register. Also there were several instances of poor people asking the Kirk Session for help in buying medicines and this was granted.

The collections from the university were to go to the poor of the parish.

Problems with illegitimate sex in St Andrews

The Kirk Session was the Child Support Agency of its day and they summoned men and girls who had sex outwith marriage and rebuked them. The Kirk Session had a very limited poor budget and consequently had to try to make sure that illegitimate children were supported.

Despite any reasons for this interference or supervision of the congregation, the Kirk Session records make strange reading. In the 1870's half of all matters before the Kirk Session seem to be about pre-marital sex with the consequences of illegitimate babies. Even married couples who had an early arrival had to appear before the Kirk Session. The couples had to appear before the Kirk session and were rebuked and were then admitted to the full privileges of he church.

The wording of the record was that Miss X or Mr X had been guilty of fornication and having expressed their penitence for this offence, they repented of their sin and were rebuked and given a solemn admonition by the Kirk Session and were absolved from scandal of their sin and restored to the privileges of the church. The wording was similar with ante-nuptial fornication. There was an item in the minutes of a letter sent to the minister and Kirk Session of Dron regarding someone who had gone there after committing fornication and they were being followed up.

The practice of summoning men and girls before the Kirk Session appears to have been less common (there were usually about two per year in the 1890's) and died out completely in 1899. The last record of this practice was on 4 December 1898. There are no records in the time of the new minister, Rev Patrick Playfair.

One man, who was a photographer, refused to appear before the Kirk Session and asked that his name be removed from the church roll. Accordingly, the Kirk Session removed his name from the roll.

General Assembly

Ministers in St Andrews Presbytery went to the General Assembly every six years at that time. Dr Boyd did not go to the General Assembly in 1876 because he was unhappy about the conduct of the Assembly and said they were intent on crushing a man. He thought he could do more good at home. Nevertheless he went to the General Assembly of 1888 and found it changed. When he was made Moderator in 1890, he took with him one of the younger elders, Mr Grace. (Presumably the same Mr Grace, that was later to help with the rebuilding of the church) Mr Tulloch (son of the Late Principal of St Mary's) was his chaplain.

Elders.

There were 56 Elders.

Some of these were:

Dr Lindsay, Balmungo (died 1878)

Sir Alexander Kinloch

Mr Whyte Melville, Mount Melville

Dr Watson Wemyss, Denbrae (died 1879)

Old Tom Morris

Principal William Tulloch (died 1886)

Provost Walter Thomas Milton (Senior elder) He died in December 1893.

New elders were often needed and nineteen elders were ordained and one elder already ordained was admitted on May 18 1890.

Sunday Schools

Before the halls were erected the Sunday Schools met in Madras College and at Greenside Place. There was an annual Christmas treat for Sunday school children. There were problems with accommodation for the Sunday school children as Madras College was not large enough. It was decided to schedule the Sunday school in the afternoon in Holy Trinity, as this was the only building large enough to accommodate the Sunday School. A new Sunday School hall was but in Greenside Place in 1903.

Events around St Andrews 1870-1895

Fishermen were drowned near the shore on October 21 1870. They could not swim. This was a common occurrence among fishermen, as they were fatalistic.

The Cathedral cemetery was extended in 1877, as the old cemetery next the cathedral was almost full. Some of the gravestones in the Cathedral Cemetery belonged to Holy Trinity church and the congregation cleaned these. (It is curious as to why the church owned the stones)

28 December 1879 was the date of the Tay Rail Bridge Disaster. The Tay Railway Bridge fell down in a storm on 28 December 1879, taking a train with it. All fifty-nine passengers were drowned including two young men from St Andrews who were members of Holy Trinity. They were going to Dundee after spending a weekend at home so that they could be at their work in Dundee at 6 a.m. on Monday morning .One of the two men was married with a young child.

To aid the local fishermen, a Fisher Bazaar was held in September 1885.

On January 6 1894, there was 20 degrees of frost. Many water pipes were frozen.

At the old folks treat in the Town Hall on December 27 1894, for the first time since the treat began, there was roast beef and plum pudding on the menu.

Some special church events

In July 1884, a service for the volunteers was held with Brass Band playing. 3000 people were present.

The Kirking of the new Magistrates was held on Sunday 8 November 1885. Dr Anderson preached the sermon. Many of the magistrates returned for the 2 p.m. service. This event was held regularly after local elections until the local government reorganisation of 1975.

Royalty also attended church. On September 5 1886, Princesses Victoria (aged 18) and Louise (aged 19) (daughters of Edward VII and Queen Alexandra) were at church.

In 1897, a service for the Diamond Jubilee of Queen Victoria was held. The hymn "O King of Kings was sung". The poorer members of the congregation (163 people) received ½ lb. of tea, 2 lb. of sugar and a 4d loaf. This was paid out of the coal fund. The children received Jubilee mugs.

Congregational parties were held in 1886 and 1887. They lasted from 7-10.45 p.m. 1600 people attended. At the tea party in 1890, Principal Cunningham spoke and Rev McGregor (St Mary's College) spoke for one hour. Not a very exciting tea party. The choir also had a party in January 1891 when 100 attended (presumably including partners) and there was even music, singing and dancing.

Fife Light Horse attended the Morning Service on July 20 1890. 2500 people were present. This was the fourteenth time their Band played in church. Services were held also in 1891 and 1892.

The yearly volunteer service was held on Sunday April 9 1893. The Brass Band played before the Artillery met the Rifles in Madras College. The trumpet played and the hymn "Onward Christian Soldiers" was sung. 2500 attended the service.

Nineteen elders were ordained on May 18 1890 and one elder already ordained was admitted to the Kirk Session.

Dr Boyd was to go on holiday on June 12 1892. In the morning, he preached on the Blessed Trinity and the service ended at 12.20 (Victorian services were not so long as often thought). He took the afternoon service, which finished at 3.10 and then visited the Sunday School.

On Christmas Day 1892, the Te Deum sung for the first time in Holy Trinity, but it had been sung previously in St Marys. The Innocents Day Text was "And a little child shall lead them."

Dr Boyd had been on duty at both services for twenty-nine out of thirty one Sundays and on the missing two he preached in Glasgow and Edinburgh

(June 1893). One of the elders said that he should go away sometimes and let the congregation see the difference.

Dr Boyd had some help however. In January 1895, at the afternoon service, a licentiate took the prayers, a divinity student gave the readings and Dr Boyd preached.

The church was decorated for the first time at Christmas 1894. The text of the sermon was "Now let us go even unto Bethlehem."

There were 40 (one communion) First Communicants in 1890, 50 in 1891, 41 in 1892, 79 in 1893, 95 in 1894, 65 in 1895, 78 in 1896, 62 in 1897, 50 in 1898 and 96 in 1899.

The Sunday School party was held on December 28 1894.

There were seven professors of the University who were members of the Kirk Session in 1895.

University events concerning the church

March 1876 Baird lectures on Theism were started in March 1976. Professor Flint (Moral Philosophy) was the first lecturer.

1889 Gifford lectures started in 1889: Andrew Lang was the first Gifford lecturer.

The eminent Free Church professor Edward Caird, who was interested in the philosophy of Hegel, gave one of the Gifford lectures. Dr Boyd wrote, "one feels an unfeigned reverence for the man, which grew week by week as he went on. If I had merely wished to be interested and stimulated or (as I heard illiterate souls express it) to enjoy an intellectual treat, I should have been more than satisfied. But I went to be helped and I was not. Dr Boyd saw through the philosophy of Hegel and it was soon to wane in Scottish theological faculties.

Cottage Hospital

Principal Shairp of St Andrews University who died on 18 September 1885 donated this. He often visited the hospital and conducted short services there, although he was not a clergyman.

Some odd property matters

Holy Trinity church had various pieces of property given on behalf of the poor of St Andrews and maintained by the Kirk Session he following are some curious items;

The Kinness burn overflowed frequently in Victorian times (and the present day). Repairs were needed to the bank, which cost £3 and £1 extra.

Law Park house needed repairs to the outside toilet. The Kirk Session agreed to repair the roof but said that the tenant should repair the toilet.

The Town Council wished to rent a piece of land between the Lade Braes and the Kinness burn as a skating pond. This was agreed.

The sewage outfall between Fleming Place and the Sea caused flooding problems to a piece of land owned by the church.

Some stories of Dr Boyd's time in the church

1 Story of the trees

There were two little twisted elms in front of the church and the heritors ordered that the two elms should be cut down to make room for two good lime trees which were fifty feet high. On Thursday April 16 1893, the two ministers rushed out of the church to find that the workmen had cut down the lime trees and left the elms. The two ministers were angry.

2 Story of the drunk woman

A drunk woman stopped Dr Boyd and asked for 2/6. He said you can have it if you come sober tomorrow to see me. She said "Ah you are just a drap doon frae Principal Haldane."

3 The address

On January 17 1893, Dr Boyd received a letter addressed "The Right Honourable and Most Reverend Lord Archbishop of Cupar. "

4 The poor sermon

A woman (in Dr Boyd's congregation) heard a dreary sermon. Who was the minister? Oh that was one of the men that mak the ministers. Deed, he must be a good man. There is no one of his students that doesn't preach far better than himself.

Dr Boyd died of accidental poisoning on 1 March 1899. He had taken a poison, which he mistook for medicine. The Kirk Session minutes records his death as "a great loss."

Dr Boyd's ministry

Dr Boyd was one of the most influential ministers in the history of Holy Trinity. His aim was to improve the worship of the church by introducing hymns and instrumental music and by proper prayers, which he preferred to read. He also wished to have services on the major holy days such as Christmas and Good Friday. These things (except read prayers) are nowadays common but they were very controversial in Victorian times and were introduced gradually, usually at St Mary's in the first instance.

The best tribute came from a member of the congregation who spoke to a visitor" never heard the doctor before. Well you are in for a rare treat."

Mark Louden Anderson MA DD

Mark Louden Anderson MA DD was born on 24 May 1829 at Caerlaverock and obtained the degree of BD (St Andrews) in 1854. St Andrews Presbytery licensed him on 16 June 1858. He was Assistant at Montrose in 1858. He was the Minister of Menmuir in Angus 1858-1875 and was admitted on 22 July 1875 to the Second Charge of Holy Trinity and was minister of the Second Charge between 1875 and 1902. He graduated DD in 1886. He was the first minister to be elected by the congregation after the abolition of patronage on July 22 1874. Women and adherents could vote as well.

There is no record in the Kirk Session minutes of the vote if any. However an attempt was made to find out who were the communicant members of the church, with a search of the records as far back as 1868.

Dr Anderson was given high praise for his ministry. "He was an upright and a downright man." Dr Boyd praised his helpfulness and kindliness. He cooperated with Dr Playfair, who held him in very high regard, in what could have been a very difficult situation. He was married. He did not live in the Manse in South Street, but owned his own house.

During 1902, Dr Anderson wished to retire, but the Kirk Session were reluctant to support this. At the Session meeting in November 1902, Rev Patrick Playfair said that he visited Dr Anderson and found him in bed and he was very weak and frail. The retiral came too late, as Dr Anderson died on 25 December 1902.

Chapter 8
Twentieth century
Introduction

The two largest Presbyterian churches, the Church of Scotland and the United Free Church of Scotland were united in 1929. The United Free Church came into existence over the rights of members to elect ministers, rather than the patrons nominating whom they liked, without regard to the wishes of the members. After this wrong was remedied in 1874, the separate existence of the churches was no longer meaningful or necessary.

But the major problem of the lack of faith and the number of the unchurched was not tackled, although the Billy Graham crusade in the nineteen fifties helped to slow the decline. Nevertheless, membership of the Church of Scotland grew until 1960 when it reached 1,300,000 thereafter there were a steady decline. The church also lost the influence of the provision for the poor, with the introduction of Old Age Pensions and National Insurance. Also, Social Security was taken over by the state. The church at the end of the twentieth century is content with the spiritual development of the members, rather than alleviating poverty. Sadly it has become more bureaucratised with the headquarters and the committees of Edinburgh more powerful and more interfering with a great loss to the individual congregations.

Rev Patrick McDonald Playfair

Rev Patrick McDonald Playfair, who was born on 5 November 1858, became minister of the first charge of Holy Trinity on 17 August 1899 until his death in October 1924. He was assistant to Dr Norman McLeod at St Stephen's, Edinburgh from 1882 to 1886. He was then minister of Glencairn from 1886 to 1899.

After preaching, the congregation voted him as minister with 718 votes to 208 against.

His ministry

Dr Playfair was a very conscientious minister. On Monday, on his second week in St Andrews, he started his visitation of the whole parish and he visited every house in the whole parish.

He held a six week course in preparation for being admitted as a Communicant and interviewed every person individually although there could be as many as 50 new communicants.

In addition to these duties, he visited St Katharine's School and the Cottage Hospital and conducted services there.

In November 1899, he was chaplain to the 6th Volunteer Black Watch.

In 1900 Dr Playfair was made a member of the Royal and Ancient Golf Club and was chaplain.

He was very highly thought of as a preacher and preached before Queen Victoria and later the other members of the Royal family.

He conducted children's services on Sunday afternoons.

He was Moderator of St Andrews Presbytery in 1919 and 1920. In 1921, he was Synod of Fife Moderator.

His last services were on 14 September 1924, when he preached at both services.

Sunday School Halls

In 1900 a proposal was made to erect halls for the Sunday school. From a bazaar and sales of work a sum of £1885 was raised. It cost £200 to buy the houses, which occupied the site in Greenside Place. The building of the Sunday school halls was started in Greenside Place during July 1902. In 1902, a hall keeper was appointed for the new halls. The completed halls were opened in December 1903 and at a cost of £2530.

Special Services

One feature of this time was that special services were held for national events, usually on a weekday, as holidays were occasionally given by royal decree. Some of these services are listed below.

On 2 February 1901, there was a service of remembrance for Queen Victoria attended by 2500 people and a service was held in the church on 9 August 1902 for the Coronation of King Edward VII.

In 1902 a Masonic service was held. This is unusual today, but the Masonic Lodge and the Kirk Session then were composed of the leading persons in the town.

In 1905 a service was held for the John Knox Quarter Centenary.

During 1905 a service was held for the Centenary of the death of Nelson, a rather surprising commemoration.

On 12 March 1911, a service was held for the three hundredth anniversary of the Authorised Version of the Bible.

On St Andrews Day 1912, there was a service of commemoration for the five hundredth anniversary of the founding of the University of St Andrews.

Events in the church

A women's work party was instituted in 1899.

During the South African War (1899-1902), the congregation contributed relief funds for soldiers' families.

On 10 March 1901, a lectern was dedicated in memory of Rev A K H Boyd.

In 1904, repairs were needed at St Mary's church.

An extra 16 elders were inducted in 1904, making the number 39 elders.

In 1908, the funeral of a famous golfer Old Tom Morris took place. He was an elder for eighteen years. There was a large funeral procession to the cathedral cemetery led by Rev Patrick Playfair.

In 1912, the church was open every day. From July until September 1912, there were fifteen thousand visitors with 691 visitors on 24 August 1912.

A parish sister was introduced for the women and girls of the congregation in September 1912. This continued until the sister in 1948 resigned and was not replaced.

1912 A Girls Guildry was formed. Later this became the Girls Brigade. It still exists in 2012.

1914 Open Air Sunday Services were held fortnightly in afternoons at Balmungo.

Church buildings in the twentieth century
Rebuilding of the church

Dr Playfair was dissatisfied with the state of the church and raised the matter with the Kirk session in 1901. A meeting was held in the Town Hall on January 10 1902, chaired by the provost and a complete renovation was proposed. It was decided to institute an appeal rather than ask the heritors for money, which could have been difficult legally and accordingly an appeal was made in September 1902. Due to the efforts of the Rev Patrick Playfair and his treasurer Mr. Charles Stuart Grace, the church was completely remodelled in 1907-1909 with the intention of restoring the church to its original form. The architect for the renovations was Mr. McGregor Chalmers of Glasgow. The church galleries were removed, so extensive rebuilding of the walls was needed. Indeed, the only parts of the old church, which remained were the Tower, the West wall and some of the pillars. Some local workmen were as follows: Andrew Thom and sons, joiners, Thomas Black, slater, J M Morris, plumber and Dewar and Robertson, painters but there were also outside contractors. A new pulpit was installed in memory of the Rev A K H Boyd. To make up for the galleries an extension was built and was called the Hunter and Memorial Aisle.

The last service in the old church was held on 2 June 1907. The ministers attending were Rev Patrick Playfair and Rev W H Leatham. The Town Council attended in their robes.

The church was completed at a cost of £30,000 and the money was nearly all raised by public subscription (the Baird Trust gave a contribution).

New windows were installed and it was very fortunate that Douglas Strachan, who was a very talented stained glass artist, and also James Powell and Sons executed the work. The great east window designed by Douglas Strachan, was a particularly fine piece of work.

The remodelled church seated 1885 persons.

The rebuilt church was dedicated on St Andrews Day (30 November) 1909 at 12.15 p.m. The preacher was Rev James Robertson, Moderator of the General Assembly.

Organ

In 1900, a 2 manual organ was installed in Holy Trinity. A new pipe organ was installed when the church was renovated in 1909. It was bought from Henry Willis and Sons. It cost £1500. Eight stops were left out and these were added in 1912, through the generosity of Mrs E J Dingwall Fordyce. The organ was first played on Sunday 30 November 1909.

Arrangements during the alterations 1907-1909

During the alterations, the congregation worshipped in the newly built Sunday school halls and in St Mary's church (what is now the Victory Memorial Hall). There was a problem with the heritors, as there were less seats in the new church than the old church, only 1885 instead of 3000, but with great generosity many of the heritors, especially the country heritors, relinquished some of their rights to seats.

The West Window was added in 1914, paid for by the women of the church.

War 1914-1918

In 1914 war against Germany was declared.

There was a daily service with prayer during the war. This was discontinued in 1919. The last daily service was held on 31 May 1919.

Parcels were sent to the soldiers.

In the winter, the evening services were held in the afternoon.

The Sunday School met in the church to save heating the Halls.

In 1915 the services in St Mary's were suspended for six months. During the war in 1918, the services were suspended in St Mary's church.

In November 1918, there was coal rationing and the Sunday School was held in the church.

On 11 November 1918, the War ended.

Thanksgiving service for the end of the War was held on 6 July 1919.

St Mary's

St Mary's was disused as a regular church on 9 July 1918. The communion services in St Mary's were in February and August and it was decided to add these communion Sundays to the existing Communion Sundays of May and November. There were proposals for St Mary's to be reopened in 1921 and there were some services for a trial period including a communion service in May 1921. St Mary's was also used while Martyrs Church was being rebuilt in 1924. The pews and pulpit were sold to Kilrenny Church and installed in 1930. The church was sold in 1931 for £1200.

Post War events

During Christmas 1918, a Communion service was held. Easter Communions were held in 1918, 1921, 1923 and 1924.

The Sunday School went back to the Halls. The Sale of Work resumed.

There were organ recitals.

An election for new elders was held in 1920. The procedure was that the Kirk Session asked for names from the congregation. These were examined and names added by the Kirk Session if required. Then the edict of election was read out and the members of the congregation had an opportunity to object to these elders. Objections were unusual but during that year one of the members made various objections to the names proposed for pretty spurious reasons. The objections were not sustained and the new elders were elected.

Again in 1920 the dress for the choir was considered.

A memorial to those who died in the First World War was dedicated about 1920. The dead included the son of the minister the Rev Patrick Playfair. There is another memorial in the form of windows high up in the church depicting the regiments of the British Army.

The flag of the Fife and Forfarshire Yeomanry was handed over to the church in 1921.

Dr Playfair died at home after being admitted to the Cottage Hospital for treatment to his foot on 6 October 1924.

Summary of the ministry of Patrick Playfair

Patrick Playfair was one of the leading ministers of his generation. He spent his time in faithful service to the people of St Andrews where he was a noted preacher. A volume of his sermons was published in 2008 entitled the "Town Kirk." A complete collection of his sermons in Holy Trinity are now in the University Library Special Collections.

James Wallace MA BD

James Wallace MA BD was born on 23 September 1871 and was minister of the second charge from 23 June 1903 until 17 May 1906. He was assistant at St Mary's, Edinburgh and was ordained at Eyemouth on 4 August 1899. After three years in St Andrews, he was translated to Inveresk on 17 May

1906, but only lived for a few months in his new charge. He died on 4 October 1906. He was unmarried.

He was very highly thought of by Dr Playfair who spoke of him as follows:

"No better and kinder colleague, no more faithful and energetic minister ever filled the second charge than Mr Wallace. We should be thankful for the years he spent among us and we should take to heart the lesson of his life and death. How much may be done. It is not how long we live, but how we employ the days given to us that tells. What effect may be won in those three brief years James Wallace has taught us. "

William Harvey Leatham MA BA

William Harvey Leatham MA BA was born in Belfast on 16 July 1875. He gained the degree of BA from the Royal University of Ireland in 1896 and MA of Belfast University in 1911. He was licensed by the Presbytery of Belfast on 30 May 1899 and was minister of the first Presbyterian Church of Londonderry from 1899 to 1901. He was at Inversnaid in 1901 and Wester Coates, Edinburgh from 1901 to 1903. He was translated to Reston on 19 March 1903 and was Minister of the Second Charge of Holy Trinity from 29 November 1906 until 15 May 1913. He was then translated to Holburn Parish Aberdeen on 15 May 1913. He was a chaplain to the Forces from 1916 to 1918 and was translated to Helensburgh West church on 19 March 1919 and completed his ministry in St Andrews, Ottowa, Canada, where he was admitted in 1929. He wrote "The Comrade in White" (1916), "The House with two gardens" and "The life of St Francis of Assisi" (1926). He died in 1937.

James Alan Cameron Murray MA BD

James Alan Cameron Murray MA BD was born in Leven on 5 March 1886 and graduated MA in 1907 and BD in 1910. The Presbytery of Edinburgh licensed him on 10 May 1910. He was then assistant at St Giles. He was minister of the Second Charge of Holy Trinity from 25 September 1913 until 17 August 1915 when he was translated to Park Parish Church, Glasgow. He demitted from Park church on 2 February 1932. He was translated to Grangemouth Kerse on 31 May 1935 and then translated to Edinburgh Tolbooth St Johns on 15 October 1943 and demitted 31 December 1954. He wrote "An Introduction to Christian Psychotherapy. (1938) " and the "Fundamentals of the Ministry of Healing" (1954).

William Kenneth Grant MA

William Kenneth Grant MA was born on 13 July 1883 and was licensed in April 1908. He was Assistant at St Bernards, Edinburgh and was ordained at Edrom on 15 December 1911. He was translated as minister of the second charge of Holy Trinity on 6 January 1916 and ministered until 24 June 1924. He joined the forces as a chaplain in 1916 and was in France with the huts and canteens for the forces and took part in the landing at Salonica. He was in Macedonia in August 1918. He was away on duty in the Armed forces until 1920. He had a bad accident when in the forces and was unable to work for six months after he came home in May 1920.

On 24 June 1924. Mr Grant was translated to Cavers. He graduated DD from Glasgow in 1936. He retired from Cavers on 31 October 1954.

An election was held for the vacancy in the second charge in 1924 with the results Rev Alexander Dunlop for 318 against 1.

Because of the death of Mr Playfair, an election was held in January 1925 for the vacancy for the first charge. The results were Rev S J Sibbald for 315 against 638.

A new election was held in February 1925. The results were Rev A S Dunlop for 967 against 62. Rev A S Dunlop was elected.

Alexander Slater Dunlop MA BD

Alexander Slater Dunlop MA BD was ordained in 1908 and was minister of Luss. He was inducted to the second charge on 9 October 1924 and translated to the first charge on 16 April 1925 after the death of Dr Playfair. He was unmarried. On medical advice, Rev A S Dunlop demitted the First Charge on 30 September 1947. He died on 1 May 1950.

In the vacancy in 1947, Rev Charles Armour assisted.

For the vacancy in the second charge the results were John Wilson Baird for 444 against 27.

John Wilson Baird MA

John Wilson Baird MA was minister of the second charge. He was educated at Glasgow University. During his university studies, he was called up for War service, when he joined the Highland Light Infantry as a combatant officer and later joined the Indian Army and was in Mesopotamia for two years. He *was* demobbed in 1919 and completed his studies. He was assistant at Inveresk church, ordained in 1923 and was minister at Kirkgunzeon 1923-1925. He was received a call to the second Charge of Holy Trinity in July 1925 and was inducted on 3 September 1925 and the Rev A S Dunlop performed the ceremony. He left for St Machar's Cathedral in Aberdeen on 26 March 1934. He was rated as a thoughtful preacher. He wrote a number of publications

An election for the First charge was held on 8 April 1948. The results were Rev W E K Rankin for 764 against 141.

William Eric Kilmorack Rankin DD

William Eric Kilmorack Rankin DD came from Cockburnspath was ordained in 1925 and inducted into the second charge on 21 February 1935 and translated to the first charge on 6 May 1948 on the resignation of Alexander S Dunlop. He was Grand Master of the Masonic Lodge between 1946 and 1947. He was rated as an excellent preacher. He received the degree of DD from St Andrews University in 1950. He retired on 31 August 1967 and died in 1976.

Bells.

On St Andrews Day 1926, the first fifteen bells, which were installed in memory of Rev Patrick Macdonald Playfair, were dedicated in 1926 in the presence of a congregation of 2000. Messrs John Taylor of Loughborough cast the bells. The bells had a total weight of 6.5 tonnes and the largest bell had a weight of 1.55 tonnes. A massive steel framework with supporting girders had to be built inside the tower. At the same time, the clock faces on the south and west walls of the tower were lowered into their present positions and some necessary restoration of the stonework was carried out. James Easson, organist of the church, played a recital of Scottish songs on the bells in the evening.

In 1938, an anonymous visitor gave the gift of two more bells. Miss Jane Mercer, in memory of members of her family gave six bells in 1962 and these were inaugurated by a recital given by John Bevan–Baker, city carillioner of Aberdeen.

Six new bells on the top of the two-octave range were dedicated on Easter Day 1998. John Taylor and Co, Loughborough, also cast these bells.

Other pre- second war matters

In 1933 new elders were elected. In 1936, new elders were required and names were suggested. There were no objections to the final list compiled by the Kirk Session. In 1939, new elders were needed and the congregation was asked to suggest suitable people. Nine new elders were elected, making a total of 37 elders.

In 1936, a memorial was erected to Mr C S Grace in the church. In 1937 Mr. Grace (son of the latter) gave two new Communion cups.

In 1936, there were thirty-one new communicants previous to one of the communions. In 1937, there were sixty-two new communicants in total.

Organ

The organ was in need of repair and The John Compton Organ Co. Ltd. carried this out in 1936 and the restored organ was dedicated on 9 January 1937.

War 1939-1945

In 1939 war was declared.

Dr Rankin was chaplain to the Army records of Officers and was called up. During the winter the second service was changed to 2.30 p.m. The church railings were requisitioned except those at the back of the church for safety. The church halls were requisitioned and the Sunday school was held in the United College hall and when this was requisitioned too, it was held in the Younger hall. When this too was requisitioned it was held in Madras gym.

The minister needed help and Mr A S Wise, Missionary to Colinsburgh Church was seconded. He resigned in 1943.

Despite the War, the church continued as usual, but numbers at Communion fell, due to men being away on service.

New communicants were admitted as usual, with thirty in 1942 and thirty-five in 1943. Four new elders were admitted in 1942.

The gates were removed for the war effort in 1943 and in the same year the evening service was changed to the afternoon, because of lighting and heating restrictions.

At the seat letting in 1943, there were 1684 sittings.

Chapter 8

Post 1945

Dr Rankin returned from the prisoner of war camp. When Rev Alexander S Dunlop retired in 1947, Dr Rankin was translated to the first charge. He wrote a book on the Pre- reformation church of the Holy Trinity.

The two charges were an anomaly by this time and it was proposed to unite the two charges but nothing happened in 1947.

There appears to be a rather long gap between Dr Rankin being translated to the first charge and Mr Armour elected to the second charge in June 1949.

An election was held for the vacant second charge. The results were as follows:

A W Abel for 136 against 740

Charles Armour for 754 against 188

Rev Charles Armour was elected.

This election happened despite seventeen elders voting to unite the charges. But the presbytery had the authority to keep the two charges.

Rev Charles Armour

Rev Charles Armour was born 2 October 1915 at Tolfield, Alberta and attended St Andrews University in 1933. He was ordained in 1938 and was minister of Buenos Aires 1939–1949 and master of St Albans' College. He was inducted on 19 June 1949 to the second charge. The church had two charges since the 16th century. Mr Armour was unpopular with some members of the congregation. These members were unwilling to accept the verdict of the election and some were so extreme that they would not attend if Mr Armour was preaching, instead preferring to walk out of the church. Sadly, some of his opponents were members of the Kirk Session, who would have been expected to support him, regardless of their personal feelings.

Mr Armour was twice Moderator of St Andrews Presbytery.

During the ministries of Dr Rankin and Rev Charles Armour, the congregation remained stationary in numbers. The communion roll rose to 2590 in 1958, but the numbers fell slightly at the Communion services and the last Communion attendance over 1000 was in November 1960. However at the retirement of Dr Rankin the congregation was still in good heart and numbered over 2000 members.

During the vacancy the question of temporary help for Mr Armour was raised. In November 1967, there was no suitable assistant available. One was available from January, but help from Professor Dickie was obtained. This caused a problem with the Presbytery Union and Adjustment Committee and eventually help from St Mary's College was obtained. Rev R. McL. Wilson was Interim Moderator in the vacancy.

When Dr Rankin retired on 31 August 1967, there was a vacancy for the first charge. The Presbytery of St Andrews wanted to unite the two charges. The matter was then discussed by the Kirk Session of Holy Trinity, who also wanted to unite the two charges, as they knew the difficult financial position and also agreed on the basis of the union of the charges. The matter was then referred to the congregation who voted by 234 votes to 166 votes to keep the two charges. St Andrews Presbytery met and there were two motions, firstly to allow the congregation to fill the vacancy and the other to refer the matter back to the Kirk Session and the congregation to review the matter. The first motion (to keep the two charges and fill the vacancy) was passed by a majority. Rev J W Patterson (Martyrs) asked that his dissent be recorded. The Church of Scotland Union and Readjustment Committee agreed to allow the vacancy to be filled. On 20 May 1968, the Presbytery agreed to allow Holy Trinity to call a minister to the first charge. The matter of the vacancy was then passed back to the congregation, who proceeded with the vacancy committee who nominated a sole nominee for the charge (Rev Dr McGlashan from Dailly church). There was a problem with endowments and it was eventually agreed to award £643 of endowments to the first charge.

Also for some reason (not in the Session minutes) Mr Armour did not apply or was not allowed to apply for the first charge vacancy as had nearly always happened previously. These decisions were to prove damaging to Holy Trinity as attendances at Communion and the numbers on the communion roll dropped significantly, during the joint ministry of Dr McGlashan and Mr Armour. The numbers at Communion were halved from the 1960's.

There were problems with the stipend of the First Charge. During the counting of the votes during the election, the Committee of St Andrews Presbytery retired and said that they could not agree with the Kirk Session on the amount of the stipend. The Kirk Session said that the resolution had been passed by them and could not be altered. A revised schedule was then made.

An election was held for the vacancy. The results were Dr Charles Y McGlashan was elected with votes for 378 votes against 118.

Rev Charles Young McGlashan

Rev Charles Young McGlashan CBE DD (1968-1977) became minister of the first charge. He was born in Paisley on 18 June 1908 and graduated MA of Glasgow University and BD in 1940. He was ordained in 1937 and was Missionary to Sheikh Othnan from 2 May 1937 to 1938. He was appointed chaplain to the Forces in 1938 and served during the war between 1939 and 1945. He was minister of Dailly between 1966 and 1968. He was inducted into the first charge of Holy Trinity in 1968. 326 communicants and 17 adherents signed the call on 26 September 1968.

Dr McGlashan asked if he was obliged to live in the manse, then at 2 Dempster Terrace. The answer was that he be not required to live in the manse.

Rev Dr McGlashan resigned due to ill health from 15 March 1977. He retired a few months later.

When Dr McGlashan retired in 1977, the two charges were united under the Rev Charles Armour.

Organ

The **organ** was reported to be in bad condition in 1960. An Organ Fund was set up in 1965 to pay for the repairs. The congregation donated £8792 in a special appeal. An application for £3000 towards the cost of rebuilding the organ was made and the organ was finally repaired in 1966 by Harrison and Harrison and rededicated on 27 February 1966. The repair cost £14,100.

Changes were made including the addition of a bombard division, donated by the family of the late Bobby Jones, the golfer, and completed in 1974.

The organ needed repairs in 2002 and this was again carried out with a contract signed in 2006 with the firm Harrison and Harrison and the work was completed in July 2008. The organ was rededicated on 12 October 2008. The work cost £135,135. The congregation raised £70,000 and an individual donor generously gave the balance so that none of the money came from the church funds. This was just as well as the congregation went ahead without the St Andrews presbytery permission.

Buildings

Various people made generous donations to the church and the congregation often gave money for a memorial to a person in the form of an improvement. In 1945, the chapel war memorial shrine was constructed with a screen, porch and furnishing. In 1948, a memorial niche was constructed. In 1950, windows were unveiled for Colonel and Mrs. Kennedy. In 1952, four lamps were installed in the Memorial Aisle in memory of Rev A S Dunlop.

The church needed constant repairs, as is usual in older buildings although 1909 is not really that old. The three constant problems were heating systems, because the church is a large building, obsolescence of equipment was also a factor and the cost of fuel was constantly rising. Lighting was often improved and sound systems are notorious for giving trouble.

The improvements and repairs can be taken together under the following headings:

Heating

In 1950, there was a new boiler installed. In 1954, the hall needed a new boiler. In 1955, there were problems with the heating of the church and halls. In 1964-5, the heating of the church was still a problem and a new meter was installed in 1964 and an accelerator in 1965. In 1965, the stove replacement cost £1760. In 1970 the heating system was changed from gas to oil. In 1971, new heating standards were set up. The heating system failed in 1982. Because of the recurrent heating problems, the services in January and February 1983 were held in the hall.

Lighting

In 1952, four lamps were installed in Memorial Aisle in memory of Rev A S Dunlop. In 1956, Mr. A G Hallum donated lamps to church, which were installed in 1957. Improvements to the lighting were made in 1966, 1968 (lighting of the roof), 1969 and 1972.

Sound

The loudspeaker system was installed in 1966 and improved in 1972. Loudspeaker systems need constant attention, although the sound is usually good in Holy Trinity.

Roof

In 1945, there was a problem with dampness in the roof. In 1947, there were repairs to the roof. During 1958, renovations cost £1538. In the early 2000s major repairs were made to the roof.

Other repairs

In 1948, the church hall platform was causing problems. During 1956, the hall kitchen was repaired and improved, costing £440. A donation towards the Carmichael windows was made in 1963. During 1964, the church hall repairs cost £1000. In 1969, repairs were made to the west front of the church. In 1970, the tower and weather vane were to be repaired. In 1972, improvements were made to the hall, paid for by the Guild.

Railings

The railings were removed during the War, replaced at an unknown date and renovated in 2004.

Hall cleaning

There were problems with the hall cleaning in 1967. The hall had not been cleaned for some time due to the illness of Mrs. Smith. In 1975, the hall keeper's appointment was terminated and no reason was given.

Ministers stipend

1948 Second charge £550

1956 First Charge £1100 Second Charge £ 750 plus manse

1957 First Charge £1200 Second Charge £ 800 plus manse

1958 First Charge £1300 Second Charge £1000 both plus manse

1959 First Charge £1300 Second Charge £1000 both plus manse

When the new minister was due to come in 1968, the stipends had to be agreed with the Presbytery of St Andrews. In May of 1968, the Kirk Session proposed the First charge stipend should be £1600 and the second charge £1475, but the Presbytery failed to agree with the Kirk Session and suggested £1590 for the First Charge stipend. The Kirk Session stuck to their original figures. The Presbytery then withdrew from the negotiations. They came back and said that they could not agree with the Kirk Session's figures. Eventually (in August) an agreement was reached with the Kirk Session agreeing that the first charge minister should be paid £1600 rising to £1800 in 1972 by £50 instalments. The Kirk Session was to make every effort to raise more money.

During all the discussion the Kirk Session had paid the second charge minister their own (and higher) figure of a stipend and this could not be reversed.

Poor fund

This fund was the result of previous donations to help the poor in St Andrews. Unfortunately because of inflation, it meant that there was not a lot of money to be distributed.

The amounts were as follows:

£89 and six shillings in 1951, £89 and 8 shillings in 1952, £89 and 18 shillings in 1953, £95 in 1954, £91 in 1955, £113 in 1956, £121 in 1958 and £146 in 1960.

In November 1967, poor single people only received £2. Inflation had reduced the money in the poor fund.

Manses

There was a manse for the church in the sixteenth century and in the early seventeenth century, but as stated previously the ministers had a problem with an illegal occupant. Thereafter the ministers had to find their own accommodation, but an extra allowance was made. This arrangement appears to have been unusual in the Church of Scotland. Rev John Park stayed at 4 Hope Street, presumably his own house. Dr Boyd in 1865 chose to have his own house and was paid an extra allowance for doing so. His two manses were Edgecliffe for 7 years and then he eventually had a new house built near the railway at 7 Abbotsford Crescent and took possession on April 15 1873. His successor the Rev Patrick Playfair bought Arden, which is now, the University Air Squadron's premises. After Rev Playfair's death, the Rev Slater Dunlop stayed with his sister and it was not until after Dr Rankin's removal to the first charge did the question of the purchase of a manse became necessary. In 1956, the congregation considered the house at 8 Howard Place, but this was not proceeded to purchase. The actual purchase of a First Charge Manse only happened in 1958. In 1958, a new manse for the First Charge was purchased at 2 Dempster Terrace and was occupied by Rev Dr Rankin. It cost £3500. When Dr Rankin retired, and Rev Dr McGlashan was appointed, he refused to occupy the manse at 2

Dempster Terrace. Accordingly, In 1968, a new manse at Linton, 16 Hepburn Gardens was purchased for £10,000. The necessary repairs cost £2938.The old manse at 2 Dempster Terrace sold for £7750. The Kirk Session said that it was not necessary to obtain permission from the Presbytery of St Andrews to sell the manse, as they had not asked permission from the Presbytery of St Andrews to buy it in the first place.

In 1871, a house at 156 South Street was given by a donation in a will and it needed some repairs, which were made. Rev Alexander Hill was the first occupant. On Rev Hill's death his widow occupied the house and a rent was fixed as Rev Dr Anderson had his own house. In 1924, a manse for the Second charge was purchased at 17 Queen's Gardens by the congregation and the manse was owned by the congregation and not the Church of Scotland trustees. In 1960, the second charge manse was repaired. In 1972, a car park was made at the manse at 17 Queens Gardens. This became the manse for the first charge when the two charges were united.

After the retiral of Dr McGlashan in 1977, the first charge manse at 16 Hepburn Gardens was sold. The manse was then the former second charge manse at 17 Queens Gardens.

In 2004, a manse was purchased at 19 Priory Gardens and the manse at 17 Queens Gardens was sold.

In 2011, Rev Rory McLeod bought his own house in Guardbridge.

Kirk Session post war

Some of the business of the Kirk Sessions concerned appointing new elders. Eighteen people were nominated by the Kirk Session in 1946, and ten of these accepted. The Kirk Session added another three names and so thirteen members were duly ordained. Not all elders came to the Session meetings and the next year (1947) there were twenty-seven elders at a Session meeting. In 1948, eight new elders were ordained and four were admitted. These admissions were elders who were ordained at their previous congregations and moved to Holy Trinity.

The position changed in 1951 when the congregation nominated thirty members to the Kirk Session and it was then decided to ordain as elders the members with the highest numbers of votes, providing they accepted.

Until 1954 the congregation, who was told that new elders were needed and were asked to submit names to the Kirk Session, who proceeded to ordain those willing to be elders, provided that not too many names were submitted. The position in 1954 was a big and very undemocratic change from the previous position and this method has persisted until the present time. New elders were ordained in 1954 by the changed method, when a committee of the ministers and three elders were to make a list of names to be submitted to the Kirk Session for approval. The committee was to make a list of twenty names. And the nominees were to be asked if they consented. Five new elders were nominated and consented and seven others were to be asked and three consented, so a total of eight new elders were ordained in June 1954.

In March 1956, three new elders were ordained. Seven new elders were ordained in March 1958. In June 1959, six new elders were ordained. Five new elders were ordained in 1960, seven new elders were ordained in 1961 and three new elders were ordained in 1964-5. In 1968, the Kirk Session wanted new elders and the present method of nominating new elders was continued. Seven new elders were ordained in March 1969 and three new elders were ordained in December 1970. In April 1971, three new elders were ordained and seven new elders were ordained in 1977. New elders were proposed in 1984 and 1989. In 2008, thirteen new elders were ordained the largest number for some years and five new elders were also ordained in 2010. Five new elders were ordained in 2012.

Matters had changed in 1965 with a new constitution being implemented and a Congregation Board set up. In 1971, a model deed of Constitution was examined and it was adopted in 1973. The Congregational Board was abolished about 2006.

The Church of Scotland had allowed women to be inducted as elders in 1966. There were some problems in Holy Trinity with several women being nominated but were unwilling to be ordained as the first women elders. Eventually on 27 November 1979, Mrs. Wright became the first woman to be a member of Holy Trinity Kirk Session. Later several more women became elders.

There have been constant discussions about members of the Kirk Session carrying out their duties at the church. In 1970, the elders were to have a duty roster —had some of them not been taking their turn on door and collection duties? In 1980 elders' duties were discussed and an elders rota was instituted. In July of that year, the elders were requested to undertake door duties in order to help the beadle in handing out hymnbooks.

Again in 1980, two of the elders were not attending Session meetings nor were they carrying out their duties in their districts. It was agreed that the minister, Rev Charles Armour should visit them, but the outcome of the visit was not recorded.

New members

New members are critical to any organisation. The church obtained members by profession of faith, By transference from other congregations and by resolution of the Kirk Session where the person was previously a church member —not necessarily of the church of Scotland- and had no certificate. Before 1966, the preparatory service and the admission of first communicants was on the Friday prior to Communion Sunday but the admission of first communicants was changed in 1966 to the Sundays prior to Communion Sundays. The preparatory service for communion continued to be held on the Friday preceding communion. The last preparatory service during the week was held on Friday 3 May 2002 and was conducted by the Rev Charles Armour. Thereafter preparatory services for the two Communions were held on the Sunday preceding the two Communions. Weekday preparatory services had been held since the sixteenth century.

Numbers of first communicants in the past were high. In 1946, there were 65 new communicants (plus a number added by resolution of the Kirk Session), 83 (plus a number added by resolution of the Kirk Session) in 1947 and 52 in

1948. 21+ in 1949 and 113 in 1950. There were 51 new members in 1951. In 1955 there were 24+ and in 1959 25+. In 1977, there were 18 new communicants, in 1978, 23 new communicants, and 16 new communicants in 1979, and 11 new communicants in 1980 and 10 in 1983.

Special Services

Over the years, there were special services on occasions, sometimes on weekdays. On 30 November 1945, there was a thanksgiving for the end of the war in Europe. A St Andrews Day service had been instituted and this should be on 30 November, whether a weekday or a Sunday, but in 1951, it was to be Sunday 3 December. There was a service in 1952 for the funeral of King George VI. when 1600 attended. On 8 June 1953, there was a service for the Coronation of Queen Elizabeth. Pupils received New Testaments. During October 1959, Professor Baxter conducted the four hundredth anniversary service of the Kirk Session, which began in 1559, being one of the first Kirk Sessions in Scotland.

During 1955, Billy Graham preached in Holy Trinity. Many converts came forward. In 1969, Holy Week Services were to be in the evening except the Good Friday service, which was to be at 11 a.m. The inaugural Service for the Council of Churches was instituted in 1969 and in the same year, the Christmas Eve Service was to be taken by rota of the ministers.

In June 1977, there was a service for Queen Elizabeth's Silver Jubilee.

In 1978, a Watch Night Service before New Years Day was begun.

During 1982, a Golf service was instituted under the auspices of the church and the Royal and Ancient Golf Club and it was still being held in 2011.

Sunday School

The Sunday School was once one of the largest in Fife. It was started in Victorian times in places like Madras school and eventually had its meetings in the new hall erected in 1903. The Sunday school met after the church service at approximately 12.10 p.m. This time was changed in 1965 to 10 a.m. (for a trial period) instead of after the 11 a.m. service. At its peak there were about four

hundred children in the Sunday school and in 1965 there were thirty-seven
Sunday School teachers and usually three hundred Sunday School pupils. The
Sunday School – now called the Young Church is now in two parts, meeting in
the church during the 11 a.m. and 12 noon services.

Guild

The Women's Guild was set up in 1929 and was once very large with four
hundred women members at its peak. It really replaced the Women's Work Party.

The constitution changed in 1997 and it was renamed the Guild, so that
men could join but to date only one man has done so.

Communion

Communion was normally celebrated twice per year on 1 May and 1
November at special services, but nowadays it is also celebrated at Christmas,
Easter and Pentecost. In 1954, Communion Sunday was changed to 31 October
for that year only, because of early Remembrance Sunday that year. During
1965, discussion was held towards the procurement of individual Communion
cups. No action was taken. The individual Communion cups, which the church
now has, were donated by Martyrs Church.

A free bus was started to take members from the new parts of the town to
Communion. This was discontinued, but numbers at Communion fell so the free
bus was reinstated. Because of the number of cars the bus was eventually
discontinued.

In 2012, the old communion cups and the individual cups are both used.

Choir

The choir was again a nineteenth century innovation and preceded the
installation of the organ. In 1953, the robing of choir was considered. No action
was then taken but due to a donation being given, the choir was robed later in the
year. The numbers sank to just four members but has since revived and is now
about twenty members.

Donations (excluding money and church interiors)

The St Andrews Rotary Club donated a Christmas tree in 1952 and this continued annually up to the present day.

Twenty collection plates were donated in 1962.

During 1971, Miss F Carstairs donated a new silver plate.

In 1973 a gift of hymnbooks were made. A further gift of one hundred hymnbooks was donated in 1974.

Badminton club

A badminton club had been set up after the War. At its beginning it was restricted by its constitution to elders, Sunday school teachers and choir members. By 1960 it needed members, so it was proposed to remove restrictions and to allow any member or adherent to join. The changes were eventually approved. It is no longer in existence.

Items connected with St Andrews Town Council and Fife Council

In 1958, a bus stop outside church was approved. The space is now a taxi rank.

Also in 1958, Fife Council Planing Committee declared a historic interest in the church.

During 1960-1962, there was a discussion between the Town Council and the Kirk Session about the curfew bell which is rung daily except Sundays since 1412 at 8 p.m. to let the citizens of St Andrews know that it was time to be at home and off the streets. The ringing of the bell was mechanised in 1961.

In 1962 the ground outside the West Side of church was repaired at the expense of St Andrews Town Council. St Andrews Town Council also in 1962, wanted to buy old skating pond on Lade Braes. The Kirk Session queried why they wanted this land. Kirk Session took no action. The Town Council had wanted the skating rink for a swimming pool but eventually decided not to go through with it. It was surprising the church owned the old skating pond.

In 1967, the Town Council carried out floodlighting of the church.

Some Miscellaneous events 1948-2004

One of the elders, Principal Duncan was to be Moderator of the General Assembly in 1948.

Sir James Irvine, Principal of St Andrews University, an elder died in 1952

A Weekly Freewill Offering was instituted in 1953.

Because of repairs to Hope Park Church, the services with Hope Park were to be shared in 1953, but the ordinary collection was to go to Holy Trinity.

Because of the retirement of the Minister of Boarhills a suggestion was made in 1953, to link Boarhills with Holy Trinity. Mr. Armour felt that he had sufficient work with Holy Trinity.

The Council of St Andrews churches was instituted in 1965. It arranged joint services among other matters. It lasted until 2010.

A loan of the Baptismal ewer was made in 1965.

The obligations of the payment of the stipends were not met in 1968.

It was proposed to have secretarial help in 1968. It was decided that this could not be afforded. However secretarial help was provided in 1969 and is still provided in 2012.

A new Freewill Offering system was instituted in 1969.

There were to be Social gatherings in 1970.

There were to be united evening services with the other St Andrews churches for January 1971.

The church silver was to be insured in 1971.

The presbyteries of Cupar and St Andrews were united in 1976.

A social area was provided in the church near the west window in 1982.

The opening of the church during weekdays was begun in 1982 and continued in 1983 Guardians for the church during extra opening hours were recruited.

Long Service certificates presented on June 29 2003.

Organist's service was recognised in 2003 with Mr Duncan being presented with a gown and hood.

A Flower Festival was held in June 2003.

Mr Armour was ill some days after conducting the services on 27 May 2002 and during his illness, the Rev Roy Hill conducted the church services. Because of his ill health, Mr Armour demitted the charge on 1 February 2003. The final service for Mr Armour was on 2 February 2003 when the service was conducted by Professor Whyte and Dr W D Shaw and Mr Armour said the Benediction. Mr Armour died on 12 February 2004. A memorial bench was placed in the front of the church in his memory.

On the resignation of Rev Charles Armour, there was a vacancy in Holy Trinity. The presbytery was reluctant to allow a new minister so the vacancy was protracted. The congregation was only allowed to appoint a vacancy committee on 16 November 2003.

During the vacancy, the Rev Harry Gibson was Moderator, but the Rev Roy Hill, a retired minister, who was a member of the congregation, conducted most of the services. The church was eventually allowed to call a minister on tenure of five years.

Rev Rory McLeod BA MBA BD

Rev Rory McLeod BA MBA BD, who was previously a chaplain to the Forces, preached on 20 June 2004 as sole nominee and was inducted in October 2004.

Rev Ian Bradley DD was inducted as Associate Minister. He is a Reader at St Mary's College. Also the **Rev Cameron Harrison** was appointed as an auxiliary minister.

The Presbytery of St Andrews wished to link Boarhills and Dunino with Holy Trinity. After the conclusion of the five-year tenure, the Presbytery had the draft basis of a linkage with Holy Trinity. The congregations had to decide whether or not the linkage was to go ahead and if so whether Rory McLeod was to be the minister of the joint charge. The congregations met on Sunday 6 June 2010 after morning service.

Both congregations agreed to the linkage but Boarhills and Dunino did not wish Rory McLeod to be their minister although Holy Trinity members voted in favour of Mr McLeod. The matter was decided at the presbytery meeting of 30 June 2010 and Mr McLeod was given extra five years as minister of Holy Trinity (until 2014) and Boarhills and Dunino were to continue without a minister meantime.

Events since 2002

2003 Vacancy Year

During this year a number of church concerts were held

2 March Tom Duncan's recital.

23 March Renaissance Group

4 May Renaissance Singers (first Concert since 1995)

8 June Illinois Symphony Orchestra

20 June (Monday) St Johns Passion

23 July Organ recital

5 October Heisenberg ensemble

8 October Recital by Jane Parker –Smith

16 November Renaissance Group Choral evensong

23 November Recital by George McPhee, Paisley Abbey

3 December Renaissance Group

14 December Carol Service

21 December Messiah

The organist 's 40 years service was recognised and Mr Duncan was presented with a gown and hood.

Stewardship

25 May 2003 New Horizons and Stewardship Campaign started.

29 August 2003 New Horizons and Stewardship Campaign commissioning of visitors

26 October 2003 Thanksgiving for New Horizons and Stewardship Campaign.

2012 January New Stewardship campaign.

Other events

2009 Centenary of Church restoration of 1909. Several events took place.

Talks were held on four prominent persons of the church in previous years:

1. John Knox
2. Archbishop James Sharp
3. A K H Boyd
4. Patrick McDonald Playfair

24 November A Scottish Songs of Praise was held

27-29 November A Flower Festival was held

30 November A Pilgrimage Walk was held with Dr Bradley

29 November A centenary Service was held and a time capsule placed in the church with items typical of 2009.

30 November St Andrews Day civic Service.

During Rory McLeod's ministry, Evening Prayers were instituted at various times during the week. It was started on four days per week at the beginning but was later reduced to Thursdays at 5.30 p.m. and in 2012 is held on weekdays (Tuesday –Fridays) at 9.15 a.m.

A second service, which was less traditional than the main service was started on 11 April 2010. It is called the Trinity Service. It meets at 12 noon or as soon afterwards as was possible. It attracted about 140 worshippers.

Twenty-four new communicants were admitted in May 2010, the largest number for some time. Thirteen new communicants were admitted in May 2011.

Youth Work in Holy Trinity has increased with additional groups. As well as the Young Church at both services on Sunday mornings, the teenagers meet in Pizza Express for their own activities. There is an Impact Summer Mission for Primary Children and the teens have a week of activities. There is a Little Cherubs for pre-school children, an after school club for Primary children and a GIG for teenagers on Fridays as well as the long established Girls Brigade and Boys Brigade. In addition there are three youth workers in the schools, so youth work has increased more than ever before.

Other matters in 2012

Five new elders were ordained in 2012.

A Stewardship Campaign was started in 2012.

Rev Dr Bradley conducted a thanksgiving service for the Queen's Golden Jubilee on 19 February 2012. A new hymn "Jubilee sets us free" was sung and the hymn which was sung at Queen Victoria's Diamond Jubilee "O King of Kings" was also sung.

Appendix1

Pre-Reformation Vicars 1412

1412 William Bonar (vicar) (died before 1440)

1475 Sir Alexander Mathison (Curate)

1505-1509, 1511, 1514 Sir Thomas Preston (vicar)

1526-1527 Sir John Matheson (Curate)

1531 Sir Thomas Preston (vicar and dean)

1538-1539, Sir William Marshall (curate)

1539 Robert Ogilvy (Vicar)

1544 Sir William Marshall (curate)

1540 John Bonar (Vicar)

1552-1553 Sir James Portaway (Vicar)

1566.1567   Sir Robert Smith (curate) (died after 1570)

Ministers

1559 Adam Heriot

1560 John Knox

1560-1565 Christopher Goodman MA BD

1566-1579 Robert Hamilton

1578 George Black

1581-1583 Robert Pont

1584-1588 John Rutherford

1589-1590 Robert Wilkie

1590-1597 David Black

1597-1612 George Gladstanes MA

1612-1638 Alexander Gladstanes MA

1639-1662 Robert Blair AM

1662-1664 Andrew Honeyman

1665-1671 Alexander Young

1673-1679 Andrew Bruce

1680-1684 William Moore MA

1684-1689 Richard Waddell MA

1689-1690 James Rymer (Rymour)

1692-1698 Thomas Forrester

1699-1712 John Anderson MA

1712-1723 William Hardie MA

1725-1737 Alexander Anderson MA

1738-1752 John McCormick MA

1738-1764 John Hill

1768-1779 James Gillespie DD

1779-1808 John Adamson MA

1808-1819 George Hill DD

1820-1854 Robert Haldane DD

1854-1865 John Park DD

1865-1899 Andrew Kennedy Hutchison Boyd DD

1899-1924 Patrick McDonald Playfair

1925-1947 Alexander Slater Dunlop BD

1947-1967 W E K Rankin DD

1968-1977 Charles Y McGlashan CBE DD

1977-2003 Charles Armour MA

2004- Rory McLeod BA MBA BD

2005- Ian Bradley (Associate)

2nd Charge

1558-1593 John Auchinleck

1593-1597 Robert Wallace MA

1597-1606 David Lindsay

1606-1613 Joshua Durie MA

1614-1620 David Barclay BD

1621-1624 George Dewar MA

1626-1637 George Wishart MA

1642-1662 Andrew Honeyman MA

1664-1680 William Moore MA

1681-1686 Robert Honeyman MA

1686-1689 John Wood MA

1697-1700 Alexander Shields MA

1701-1712 William Hardie MA

1712-1718 Laurence Watson MA

1719-1738 John McCormick MA

1738-1753 John Hill

1753-1757 David Carnegie

1757-1765 James Gillespie

1765-1771 David Hunter MA DD

1772-1779 John Adamson MA DD

1780-1808 George Hill DD

1813-1860 George Buist

1860-1875 Alexander Hill

1875-1902 Mark Louden Anderson MA DD

1903-1906 James Wallace MA BD

1906-1913 William Harvey Leatham MA BA

1913-1915 James Alan Cameron Murray

1916-1924 William Kenneth Grant MA

1924-1925 Alexander Slater Dunlop MA BD

1925-1934 John Wilson Baird MA

1935-1947 William Eric Kilmorack Rankin DD

1949-1977 Charles Armour MA

3rd charge

1593 Robert Yuill (Reader)

Auxiliary minister

2009 Cameron Harrison

Appendix 2

Bishops from 1550 –1690

John Hamilton 1547-1571

Gavin Hamilton 1571 co-adjurer since 1551

John Douglas 1572-1574

Patrick Adamson born1537 Introduced 1574 died 1592

George Gledstanes 1604-1615

John Spottiswoode 1615-1638

James Sharp 1661–1679

Alexander Burnet 1679-1684

Arthur Rose 1684-1689

Appendix 3

Cases of witchcraft 1542-1667

1542 Payment to servants bringing witches from Edinburgh to St Andrews Castle at consent of vicar general. Expenses of burning 3 witches condemned by sentence at St Andrews.

1569 A notable sorcerer called Nic Melville (? Nick Niven) was condemned to death and burned. (Herries)

William Stewart, Lord Lyon King of Arms hanged for divers points of witchcraft and necromancy (? Trial before a civil court)

Lord Regent passing to the north, he caused burnt certain witches in St Andrews.

1572 April 28 A witch burnt, Richard Bannantyre

1575 Marjorie Smith charged and accused of witchcraft. Husband and wife fled. Husband was afraid for his wife and not for himself) (Kirk Session)

1581 Bessy Robertson charged with witchcraft (Kirk Session page 455). She was warned and ordered to go before the Session.

1588 Processes against a witch presently in prison were ordained to subscribe the same authenticity that it might be delivered to counsel in Edinburgh. (Calderwood)

1588 Alison Pearson of Boarhills, who was consulted by Patrick Adamson was condemned by the High Council.

July 17 1588 Agnes Melville daughter of the late Andrew Melville elder of Anstruther was served a writ as suspect of witchcraft. It was not proceeded against at the time.(Kirk Session page 620)

1595 September 10. Several persons discerned to make public humiliation for bringing of Agnes Melville with two other deceased witches Elspot Gilchrist and Janet Lochequair. (Kirk Session)

Unknown date Isabel Anelle and others accused of consulting with witches and sentenced to undertake public humiliation and repentance.

Unknown date "King James spent several days in St Andrews to purge the university's Presbyterians and for the trial and punishment of witches. The number of witches exceeds. Many are condemned and executed chiefly for their revolt from God by especial sacrament (as they term it) in receiving the devils mark set in their flesh and in secret part as it has been confessed by and seen in many and wherein many of several sorts are accused. They profess sundry fantastical feats to have been executed by them all which shall I think be published or I forbear to trouble you therewith." (Robert Barnes)

Unknown date Patrick Stewart suspected of witchcraft.

1598 Gillian Gray and Alison Peirie (she was illegally tortured by a laird) were accused.

1604 Jonet Small accused of witchcraft. Result unknown

1613 September3 A writ to be presented to the Archbishop of St Andrews against Agnes Anstruther suspected of witchcraft. (Synod of Fife)

1614 Agnes Anstruther and Isobel Johnstone to be proceeded against for witchcraft. (Synod of Fife)

1630 January 21 Commission to the Baillie of the regality of St Andrews and his deputes for putting of Margaret Callender to the trial of an assize for witchcraft. (Privy Council)

1643 One good lad of St Andrews for riding on a Sunday to try to persuade Lord Burghley to release his wife Margaret Balfour suspected of witchcraft, is appointed to obey what the Kirk Session shall enjoin him to do for breaking the Sabbath. (Privy Council)

1643 Six witches from various churches in St Andrews presbytery executed.

1644 Alexander Baton accused of witchcraft. Result unknown.

1644 Memo of deceased Bessie Mason, a confessing witch. (Synod of Fife)

1645 Christian Rock accused of witchcraft and died in prison, before she could be freed.

1645 Andrew Carmichael accused of witchcraft and freed.

David Zeaman, Jonette Williamson, Jonet Foggow and Beatirix Ferguson were charged with witchcraft. The result was unknown.

1645 The woman called Seweis in the prison of St Andrews suspected of witchcraft and aginst whom are strong presumptions to be diligently dealt with. (Synod of Fife)

667 January 8 Commission for trial of Issobell Key prisoner in the Tolbooth, guilty of witchcraft. (Privy Council)

Appendix 4

Organists

1882 Miss Bella Sorley

1899 Mr.George Alexander Goddard

1893 Miss Elizabeth Sorley

1897 Mr. William Duncan

1908 Mr. Ainslie Duncan

1908 Mr. Herbert Wiseman

1921 Mr. Alexander Hendry

1922 Mr. James Easson

1939 Mr. George Alison Short

951 Mr. Gordon Cameron

1960 Mr. John Fletcher

1963 Mr. Thomas Duncan

Beadles

1874 Mr. James Mitchell

1899 Mr. John Webster

1936 Mr. Alexander Webster

1961 Mr. Harry Eagle

2006 Mr. George Donaldson

Appendix 5

Bibliography

Anonymous *Tales and Sketches of the Covenanters.*

Rev Robert Blair *Robert Blair.*

Rev Dr A K W Boyd *Twenty-five years in St Andrews* 2 volumes.

Rev Dr A K W Boyd *Occasional and Immemorable Day*s Longmans 1895.

Rev Dr A. K W Boyd *Last years of St Andrews* 1895.

Rev Dr A K W Boyd *St Andrews and Elsewhere* 1894.

Julia Buckroyd *The life of James Sharp Archbishop of St Andrews 1618-1679* John Donald 1987.

Julia Buckroyd *Church and State in Scotland 1660-1681* John Donald 1980.

J B Cowan *The Scottish Covenanters 1660-1688* London 1976.

Andrew Drummond and James Bulloch *The Scottish Church 1688-1843* 1981.

J King Hewison *The Covenanters* 2 volumes Constable 1908.

Roger Kilpatrick *The Ministry of Patrick McDonald Playfair* 1930.

Dane Love *Scottish Covenanters Stories* 2009.

Dane Love *Covenanter Encyclopaedia* 2009.

Lyon *History of St Andrews*

Thomas McCrie Life *of Andrew Melville* 1823.

McDonald Witches of Fife .

Rosalind K Marshall *John Knox **2010.***

Hugh Playfair *the Town Kirk* 2008 Librario Publishing.

Hugh Playfair *the Stained glass of Holy Trinity Church St Andrews Fife* June 2009.

Rev Dr W G Rankin *The Parish Church of the Holy Trinity Pre Reformation.*

Thomas Stephen *Life and Times of Archbishop Sharp of St Andrews. London 1839 reprint*

Woodrow's *Analecta* 4 volumes.

The Parish Church of the Holy Trinity St Andrews 1992.

A New Guide to The Parish Church of the Holy Trinity St Andrews 1998.
Parish church of the Holy Trinity Kirk Session Minutes Printed 1559-1600 thereafter written (missing 1600-1638)
St Andrews Citizen Particularly papers for 2002 and 2003.

www.ingramcontent.com/pod-product-compliance
Lightning Source LLC
Chambersburg PA
CBHW031852090426
42741CB00005B/457